MANUAL OF HORSEMANSHIP

Instructions from Mexico's Renowned Escuela Ecuestre

Harold Black

The director of Mexico's great riding school Escuela Ecuestre presents the sort of advice about all aspects of horsemanship that has earned international renown for the school that he runs.

Bringing to his subject a broad knowledge of both horses and people, he makes the reader understand riding from the horse's point of view. Preparing the reader with preliminary exercises for suppling him, the instruction proceeds to leading the horse and mounting and dismounting. On the theory that it is the horse who teaches the green rider, while the wise instructor gives counsel and guidance, there is a study of the psychological and physical characteristics of the horse, followed by the concept of the balanced seat, natural and artificial aids, mounted exercises at walk and trot, basic dressage, riding in multiples, faults which a horse may acquire, use of the longe, cavalletti, gaits, jumping, and combined training. Illustrated with 35 drawings by the author and 125 photographs, this book will be invaluable in many ways to the horseback rider.

Harold Black

It was at the age of forty-four that Harold Black first engaged seriously in the sport of horsemanship. Artist, enamelist, and designer of medical and scientific exhibits, he left a promising career in New York's Greenwich Village for a quiet life of painting, writing, and learning to ride horseback in San Miguel de Allende in the state of Guanajuato, Mexico. Under the guidance of the experienced author and teacher of horsemanship, Margaret Cabell Self, he became accomplished enough to be invited to ride and train at a Mexican cavalry unit with the officers. He grew so proficient that it was inevitable that he founded his own school, and his Escuela Ecuestre has now achieved wide renown throughout the equestrian world.

Jacket design by Salem Tamer

MANUAL OF HORSEMANSHIP

Instructions from Mexico's Renowned Escuela Ecuestre

BY HAROLD BLACK

Director, Escuela Ecuestre SMA

San Miguel de Allende, Gto., Mexico

ILLUSTRATED WITH DRAWINGS BY THE AUTHOR
AND PHOTOGRAPHS BY LOIS HOBART

Jacket design by Salem Tamer

1978 EDITION

W

Published by
Melvin Powers
WILSHIRE BOOK COMPANY
12015 Sherman Road
No. Hollywood, California 91605
Telephone: (213) 875-1711

Printed by

HAL LEIGHTON PRINTING CO.
P.O. Box 1231
Beverly Hills, California 90213
Telephone: (213) 983-1105

ISBN: 0-87980-359-2
Library of Congress Catalog Card Number: 73-19083
Printed in the United States of America

To My Wife, Lois

Acknowledgments

It is seldom possible to acknowledge all the debts one accumulates in the development of skills and knowledge over a long period of time. However, I must enumerate my special obligations to:

Mrs. Margaret Cabell Self, who for well over a decade has been a generous counselor and a warm and valued friend.

For whatever equestrian skills I may possess I am particularly indebted to my mentors:

Gen. Francisco Gallegos L., Mex. Cav. Ret., who first encouraged my rather fanatical determination. Lt.-Col. Rolando Leyva V., Mex. Cav., who imbued me with courage. Capt. Roger Barceló L., Mex. Cav., who led me to seek finesse.

For sound advice on equestrian mechanics and equine physiology, I wish to thank Capt. Mariano Lejarza S., Mex. Cav. Ret. who is staff veterinarian of the Escuela Ecuestre of San Miguel Allende.

For loyal cooperation and help in teaching routine which gave me the time to write this book, I am grateful to my staff of instructors and trainers here at the Escuela Ecuestre. I particularly wish to acknowledge the help of my assistant, Juan Rojas, and of trainer-instructors Gumaro Guzmán, and Antonio Luna V., who also posed for many of the photos in this book.

The opportunity to ride intensively in many countries, to

visit, and to study schooling methods in outstanding equestrian centers of both hemispheres has been an exciting adventure. The scope of these travels has been made possible by the enthusiastic cooperation of many government officials and the generous hospitality I have enjoyed from outstanding horsemen in many countries. Again it is not possible to enumerate individually all those to whom I stand in debt, but I do wish to express my deep gratitude to the following:

H.R.H. Prince Philip of Great Britain and Lt. Col. J. M. Miller, CVO, DSO, M.C., Crown Equerry, whose generous efforts on my behalf in England and Ireland can never be repaid.

Good friend Brian Young of Crabbet Park Equitation Center in Sussex for his many kindnesses. Mr. and Mrs. Robert Hall of the Fulmer School of Equitation. Capt. James Mackie RHS/O of Her Majesty's Household Cavalry. Dal O'Toole of Canadian Pacific Airways and longtime friend. Director and staff of Stoneleigh.

Capt. Ian Dudgeon and Miss Sylvia Stanier of Burton Hall, Leopardstown, Ireland. Mr. Joe Lynam of the Irish Tourist Board. Commander and staff of McKees Barracks, the Army Riding Center, Dublin, for their warm hospitality. Mr. Willy Leahy, M.F.H., and Miss Olivia Bishop for their help in Galway.

Gen. Div. Joaquín Salano Chagoya, former Commander of the Mexican Cavalry, and Brig. Gen. Miguel Rivera Becerra, former Mexican military attaché in Paris, for their kind cooperation in arranging my reception at military equitation centers in France and Spain.

The military commanders and staff of both Saumur and Fontainebleau, whose lavish hospitality to me and my group will never be forgotten.

Similarly the commanders and staff of the Escuela de Caballería del Ejército of Spain and in particular to Capt. Arturo Guillén. Good friend Antonio Alvarez Acado of Madrid, with memories of many adventures together on horseback riding out of his installation.

Distinguished dressage master Herr Josef Neckermann for his great hospitality in Frankfurt and Wiesbaden.

Baroness Piruquet of the Reitzentrum Markhof and Mr. John Lansetter for their great kindness in Vienna and at the Spanish Riding School.

Sr. Tomaz Branquinho de Fonseca for his many courtesies at his riding center in Lisbon.

Good friend Tamas Flandorffer of Budapest for the great times we have had together riding in many parts of Hungary.

I wish to express my deep appreciation for all the friendships formed through horsemanship in general and the Escuela Ecuestre in particular.

HAROLD BLACK

Preface

The purpose of this manual is to offer an outline guide to those subjects most vital to the active horseman. The extent of the material covered precludes that any of it can be treated in depth. Specialized books are available to those riders who wish to examine more profoundly any of the various subjects here treated.

Since its founding in 1963, the Escuela Ecuestre has included a series of theory lectures for all students as part of its basic course. Experience has shown that invaluable hours of mounted work in the ring are saved if the student-rider has been given a previous explanation, with appropriate visual aids, of what may be expected of him when mounted. No mounted rider, executing what may be for him a difficult maneuver, gives the instructor the measure of attention that he gives readily when he is seatd in the classroom.

It is perhaps unfortunate that comparatively few schools of horsemanship are so constituted that they are able to include theory in their routine. Although it is possible to combine the teaching of theory with active mounted instruction, it is inevitable that much overall perspective will be lost in the process. As in many other arts, the bodily reactions and facilities required by horsemanship are largely dependent upon a mental grasp or concept of the problems involved. The various visual aids developed at the Escuela, such as the articulated horse, the dressage teaching devices, and so forth, are all directed toward the mental understanding of the horseman. It is true that no amount of mental grasp will make up for a poor seat. However, in terms of progress in horsemanship, the reverse is also true.

Over the years hundreds of Escuela students have requested that the theory lectures be put into handy reference form. This book is an answer to those requests.

Contents

MANUAL OF
HORSEMANSHIP

Introduction

In the long view of history, man's romance with the horse has been rather brief, some four thousand years or less. Coexistence of a kind has been in effect for over thirty thousand years and possibly much longer. Cro-Magnon man was keenly aware of the horse, as we know from the Lascaux Cave paintings and others in southern France and Spain. Whether the horse stirred his heart or only his hunger, we cannot say. Evidence in these same paintings indicates that the horse was then an object of the chase and was hunted for food. Relations have improved considerably in the intervening years.

The valley of the Tigris and Euphrates rivers, which cradled so much of ancient civilization, was also probably the scene of the first domestication of the horse. Somewhere between 2000 and 1500 B.C. the horse began to take the place of other beasts of burden in pulling wheeled carts and finally war chariots.

The first known treatise on the care and schooling of the horse was cut in cuneiform tablets by Kikkulia the Hittite in 1440 B.C. It makes no mention of riding the horse. We can but attempt to picture that first bold dreamer who threw a leg over one of these creatures and rode.

It was at that obscure moment of history that man's complicated relations with the horse were born. This time we know that the heart of man *was* stirred, and if his hunger was aroused, it was not for food but for an experience partly of physical exhilaration—the thrill of dominating or becoming one with a strength many times his own—partly esthetic and mystic, and partly composed of elements which present-day psychologists have not yet finished studying.

It remained for the Greeks to leave us two symbols that, examined from the vantage of history, shed considerable light on man's conscious and subconscious view of the horse. One is Pegasus, the winged horse, born full grown from the blood of Medusa when she was slain by Perseus. Is it coincidence that Pegasus was the steed of the Muses, the vehicle of poetic inspiration? Or is not the horse himself one of nature's expressions of fluid poetry? In one respect Pegasus represents the most romantic and just *quid pro quo* of history. The horse gave wings to man—ergo, give wings to the horse.

The other Greek equine symbol is the Centaur, half man, half horse, capable of incredible feats of strength and speed. If Pegasus represents the esthetic aspect of the horse, then Centaur represents the power and lure of his animalism (and was so regarded by the Greeks). But there is something more here, and the Greeks did not speak of it. Centaur symbolizes the object of all genuine aspirations to horsemanship—to be as one with one's mount. In Centaur, man and horse are irrevocably joined as one being.

We will not attempt any serious investigation of the psychological ties that bind man and horse. The fact that he holds a mysterious fascination for many humans has enabled him to survive into the age of jets.

His popularity for sport and art is on the increase in most civilized parts of the world and especially so in highly industrialized and mechanized cultures.

It is apparent that in the centuries of their relationship, man has had a considerable influence on the evolution of the qualities of the horse. What is less often discussed is how much influence the horse has had on the evolution of human society. It may be profitable to ask, who has influenced whom more? A fair case can be made for the conclusion that no other single creature has so affected the forms of society up until the beginning of the twentieth century, and well after.

The horse's functions up to our own century may be roughly divided into work, war (and the sports or games directed toward that end), and transportation. In each of these spheres the pattern of human society was modified and adapted to the horse's basic needs, characteristics, abilities, and limitations.

The horse as work animal has probably exerted the least influence on human life. Long before he pulled the plow it was being hauled by oxen, asses, quaggas, or other domestic beasts. It was in the spheres of war and transportation that the horse became a silent but potent director of human ways of life.

It has most likely been more than four millennia since the first war horse was hitched to a chariot in Mesopotamia. Ever since that time, and into the atomic age, the concept of warfare, which has unfortunately occupied so much of human endeavor, has been largely molded by his use. The United States abolished its horse cavalry in 1942 during the Second World War. The armored forces that took its place were considered cavalry. All the knowledge achieved in the use of cavalry was to be incorporated into the direction and function of this armored force.

We approach our future precipitously. We explore the moon. But in our daily life and thought, the past is a more compelling directive than is our vision of the future. Only seventy years ago, the greater part of the world's short transportation was by horse; the railroads were the only serious contenders for long hauls. It is mainly the internal combustion engine and the growth of automobile travel that have emancipated the horse from the basic job he has patiently performed for centuries. It is only the advent of the rocket that has given us a new conceptual term for motive power. Until the term "thrust" entered the language, our measurement of impulsion or drive was—and still is—horsepower.

Up to and into the present century, one of the chief fashion dictators of human clothing was our friend the horse. Riding attire is now completely separated from our daily clothing, but that is a recent development. It is a conservative realm of fashion that changes little because it is functionally determined, as has been most riding apparel throughout history. The human and horse armor of the medieval knight, awkward in the extreme, was still functional to the task intended.

The horse at his best is himself a dashing and romantic creature. Since ancient times much of this dash and glory has brushed off onto the rider. The *chevalier* in France is a bold and noble gentleman. In Spain and Latin America *"caballero"* distinguishes a gallant gentleman. He may never have ridden a horse, but he is expected to exhibit those attributes of nobility that formerly marked the horseman.

In most areas of life as it evolved in Europe, Asia, and the northern countries, we find it adapted to the horse. It is reflected in architecture, city and village planning, roads and communications, location of inns and smithies, and a hundred other facets of daily living. The huge medieval courtyard was a parade ground and rallying point for horses. In times of siege the horse was part of the enclosed population of defenders. When he sallied forth he did so through portals, over moat and drawbridge designed for his needs and use.

It was in the fifth century B.C. that large groups of Asian horsemen first came into contact with European foot soldiers. This posed a critical problem for Philip of Macedon and later for Alexander. From that time until August, 1914, the use of the horse was the dominant factor in the science of war.

We may well ask at this point, "How would man have developed without the horse? What kind of civilization would have evolved?"

Fortunately, history has given us not only a perfect example of this contrast but a demonstration of what resulted when a horse civilization came into armed conflict with a horseless one.

In 1519 the Aztec empire of Mexico was at the peak of its

fairly recent power. The conquistadors of Cortez's small band could only marvel at the complexity and efficiency of their social order, the magnificence of their architecture, and the abilities of their artisans. Tenochtitlan had more than a thousand street cleaners, a sharp contrast to the predominantly filthy European cities of the period. Its architecture, canals, and aqueducts so dazzled the Europeans that according to Bernal Diaz they agreed that no city of Europe could remotely compare with it, including Venice, which some of the Spaniards had seen.

The civilizations of Mexico, as in the rest of North and South America, had evolved not only without horses but without beasts of burden of any kind, unless the llama of Peru is excepted. The contrast between the Aztec and Spanish administrations of empire is revealing. All Spanish possessions were incorporated into the political machine and culturally assimilated, if possible. The only communication the Aztecs had with their outlying empire was an elaborate series of relay runners and, of course, foot soldiers on the march. With their subject peoples the Aztecs attempted neither to assimilate nor incorporate them politically except to the extent of demanding and receiving tribute in the form of goods, slaves, and human sacrifices.

The conquest of a vast empire by a relatively few Spanish foot soldiers, cavalry, and Indian allies is one of the miracles of history known to every schoolboy. "After God, we owed the victory to the horses!" said Cortez.

The most interesting fact to us is not that the horsemen prevailed but that there was such an enormous difference between a society with and without horses. These differences extended to dress, religion, social organization, political administration, architecture, town planning, and communication. We cannot say how many of these essential differences were due to the absence of horses, but that many were, is an inescapable fact.

And so we conclude that for four thousand years the

horse has been influencing the life of man to the best of his silent ability. But how long has man been influencing the development of the horse to the best of *his* ability?

In some parts of the world, controlled breeding and some knowledge of genetic factors are centuries old. But it is only in the last fifty years that the horse has ceased to be a necessity and become primarily a vehicle of sport and art. In the next four millennia of their association, how much will man influence the horse? Through greatly increasing knowledge of genetics and a growing interest in the science and art of horsemanship on the part of man, the horse may at last be free to attain undreamed of triumphs in the future.

I

Horsemanship

Why study horsemanship?

At first glance this question may seem superfluous. A short examination of the world scene will show that it is not.

We are talking about one of the fastest-growing sports in the world. More and more people want to ride, especially in highly industrialized countries. This is a natural desire to escape, when possible, from the more synthetic aspects of industrialized life. But with more and more people in need of instruction, really knowledgeable instructors seem to be scarce.

As recently as thirty years ago, most countries maintained sizable cavalry forces; the Second World War wrote "Finis" to that. The function of these cavalry forces was more than military—they formed a constantly replenished reservoir of equestrian knowledge. It was their business to keep up with advances in such knowledge, always to try to ride better. They formed the backbone of civilian riding, of polo, and of all forms of jumping competition. They also formed the core of most teaching.

A quarter century ago, by far the greatest proportion of Olympic equestrian competition came from cavalry officers. Now the civilians have perforce largely taken over. This does not imply that the standards of Olympic competition are lower now than they were then. The contrary is true.

It does imply that there was then a generous breed of

cavalry-trained instructors available to civilian riders of all
levels, which is not now the case. With so many competent instructors around, the incompetents found it hard to survive.
Not so today. Almost anyone can acquire a few horses and
hang out his shingle as a riding instructor. If he wished to
teach people to fly airplanes, several branches of the government would take a keen interest in his competence, his facilities,
and the condition of his aircraft.

Since he wishes only to teach people to ride horses, he is at
liberty to make any claims of competence that people will
believe, whether actual or imagined. If there is no other facility
nearby, people may well continue to come to him simply because there is no place else to go.

In England the British Horseman's Society has made valiant
efforts to investigate, inspect, and approve or disapprove any
establishment that purports to teach riding. In the United
States and Canada this is not the case.

There is a common phenomenon that I have observed with
some amazement. Fourteen-year-old Lisa is "horse-happy," as
are many girls her age. She begs Mommy and Daddy for a
horse.

Logically, Lisa should be given riding lessons under a
competent instructor. When she has developed some basic
skills, and if her parents can afford it, she should have a horse,
which should be purchased with the help of someone who
knows something about the subject.

This seldom happens. More often than not, to stop Lisa's
crying, the parents rush out and buy the first nag that appears
to be a bargain. Of course the horse knows little more than
Lisa does. But Mommy and Daddy have decided that Lisa and
"horsie" will learn together. They will teach each other.

It just doesn't happen. Lisa takes off bareback at the
gallop with her little girl friends taking turns climbing up
behind her. The day after Lisa's first fracture is set, the horse
gets sold.

The same parents would be far too sensible to buy Lisa
a Thunderbird and send her out on the highway to learn to

drive. In a way, though, it might be safer. The Thunderbird does not have a mind of its own. It might not be too difficult for Lisa to turn off the ignition. Turning off the ignition on an excited or frightened horse is sometimes more complicated if one hasn't learned how.

When we come to the skills of adults, I can only repeat the kind of observation I have been hearing again and again: "I've been riding off and on for years, but I really don't know what I'm doing. Now I've joined the hunt and I've had three bad falls. I thought I'd better come down here and get some intensive lessons."

It's never too late! One is never too old! But it is far more sensible and by far more satisfying to learn first to ride under

Fig. 1: The parts of the horse (Escuela Ecuestre articulated horse)

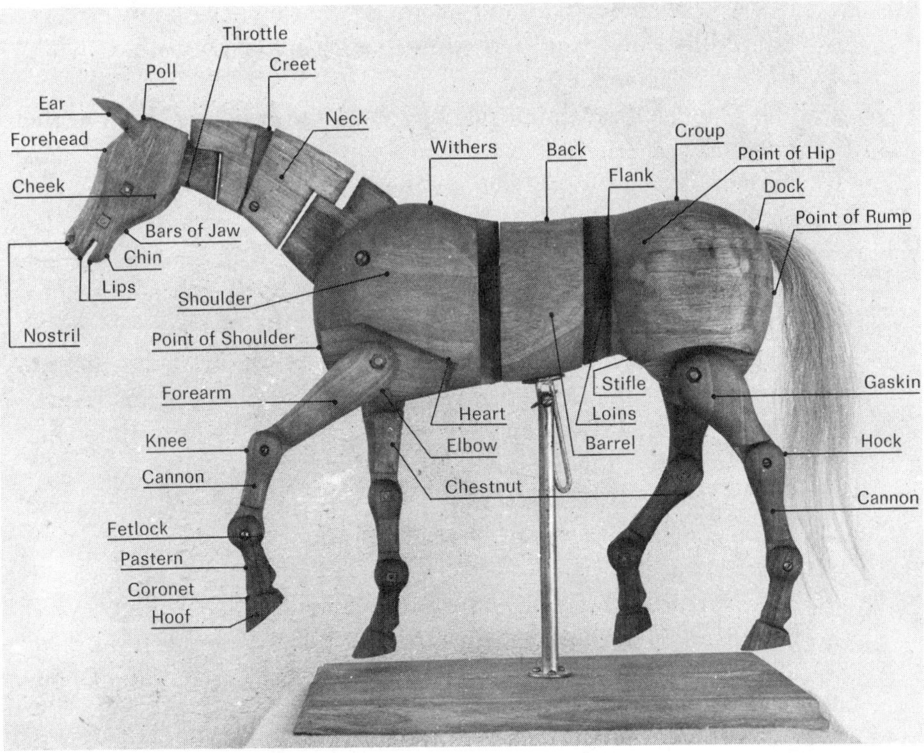

Throttle
Creet
Poll
Ear
Neck
Forehead
Withers
Back
Croup
Cheek
Flank
Point of Hip
Dock
Point of Rump
Bars of Jaw
Chin
Lips
Shoulder
Nostril
Point of Shoulder
Forearm
Stifle
Gaskin
Heart
Loins
Knee
Elbow
Barrel
Hock
Cannon
Chestnut
Cannon
Fetlock
Pastern
Coronet
Hoof

controlled conditions. Many people have been frightened for life out of jumping by being suddenly confronted with a fence with no adequate preparation, either physical or psychological.

Riding, like other human endeavors, entails the pragmatic experience of centuries and is a body of knowledge that can be imparted by a capable teacher who is also motivated.

The wise instructor gives counsel and guidance. Pragmatically, it is the horse and the horse only who teaches the green rider!

For this reason a green or even intermediate rider can never be taught a given exercise *if the horse under him has not been taught the exercise first.*

It is not possible to teach jumping except on a horse that has been taught to jump properly. Not even the basic elements of dressage can be taught on a horse that has not learned them.

An instructor who has at hand horses whose knowledge is limited to walk, trot, and canter can teach exactly that: walk, trot, and canter.

The task of training school horses and bringing them to the point of real usefulness for teaching is not economic, but it is a reality I have found has no short cuts. The green horse purchased for school use, with rein and bit, and knowledge of walk, trot, and canter, will need approximately six months of intensive schooling before he is ready for his first student. The absolutely green horse will need six months to a year or more of intensive schooling before he is ready for his first student. During this time the horse will not earn one cent of income.

A particularly adaptable horse will require less time and a particularly difficult horse much more.

In any case the economic reality is that few schools are so organized that they can offer the student the horse necessary to learn on.

When first learning lateral movements, the average green rider is inept and uncoordinated. The horse under him must be an expert at the two-track in order to interpret the rider's confused signals.

However, by trial and error he will advise the rider when he is finally applying the correct aids.

You will naturally be drawn to any school or instructor by reputation. If you have found a capable, knowledgeable, and patient instructor, you will be in good hands. He should not merely impart imperative orders, he should be willing and able to explain why one method of riding is better than another.

The next question you may ask is, "What can the horses do?"

II

Preliminary Exercises on the Ground for Suppling the Rider

A. PURPOSES

1. To develop and maintain in the rider a physical condition suitable to riding and thus adapt him physically to those movements of the horse *which must be followed by the rider.*

2. To eliminate those defensive reactions of the body that are involuntary since they are based on the unconditioned reflex. Each distinct sport makes a different set of demands upon the body, often implying a different set of muscles. (The demands of ballet dancing, for instance, are so distinct from those of horsemanship that many ballet masters forbid serious ballet students to ride intensively.) On the other hand, ballroom dancing makes many demands similar to those of horsemanship.

The early bodily defenses against the demands of horsemanship, based on the unconditioned reflex, prevent the physical relaxation of the rider that is the first requisite of all good riding. The tenseness of any portion of the rider's anatomy is instantly apparent to any experienced instructor, but it is even more quickly sensed by the horse, who reacts by various *equine defenses.*

3. To develop equilibrium, the faculty of man to adapt his body to motion, voluntary or imposed, in order to maintain

12

stability and balance. The unconditioned reflex we employ in walking (the swinging of the arms as counterbalance) is a type of reflex which is *inimical to riding*.

Equilibrium in riding implies the ability of the rider to displace—forward, backward, or laterally—in order to both *accompany* the horse and *influence* him. We say that a rider is *left behind* when his lack of bodily fluidity prevents him from going *with* the horse.

4. To develop *independence* in the various members of the body so that a voluntary motion of one part will not set up a responsive but *involuntary* reaction on the part of another member of the body. (On approaching a fence, the necessary application of the impulsor legs should never result in the bouncing of the hands or the flapping of the elbows.)

B. APPLICATION OF EXERCISES

They are useful for all riders. They are not limited to the green rider. On the contrary, they may be made more demanding for the advanced or professional horseman.

Although the basic ones here given have general application, the knowing instructor will devise individual exercises to deal with individual characteristic faults demonstrated by different riders.

Since the ankle plays so important a role in equitation, it is worthy of special comment here. It is the cushion of all reactions that the rider receives from the horse. In the case of a green rider it will largely be the facility of his ankle that will determine what he can do. The rider who must exaggeratedly force his ankle in order to keep it down will merely inhibit his riding. What is essential is the ability not only to keep the heel down but to keep it down relaxed, loose, and ready to do its proper work. The relaxed ankle will enable the rider to apply the leg behind the girth, *keeping the heel down*. In the case of the rigid ankle, the application of the leg usually results in the *raising of the heel* and thereby the loss of influence.

C. EXERCISES

1. Standing at attention, slowly and rhythmically turn the head to the right, up, left, and down. This rotation of the head serves to loosen the muscles of the neck (fig. 2).

Fig. 2: Exercise # 1

2. With the legs slightly apart, do a rotation of the waist slowly and rhythmically with arms completely loose. This will serve to improve balance and give softness to the shoulders (fig. 3).

3. Supporting yourself with the hands on the ground and legs extended, raise yourself on the points of the toes, flex the arms until the chest touches the ground. This serves to improve the position of the back (fig. 4).

4. On the knees with hands supporting yourself on the

Fig. 3: Exercise # 2

ground, slide this way little by little, until the chest touches the ground, at the same time raising the head. This exercise will give elasticity to the vertebrae (fig. 5).

5. Standing at attention, rhythmically raise one leg toward

Fig. 4: Exercise # 3

the rib cage. This will serve to loosen the hip and enlarge the crotch (fig. 6).

6. Standing at attention, open the legs laterally and flex forward until you can touch the toes with the fingers. This both enlarges the crotch and gives elasticity to the waist (fig. 7).

7. Standing at attention, raise one foot and rotate it from the knee down. This will give looseness to the articulation of the ankle (fig. 8).

Fig. 5: Exercise # 4

Fig. 6: Exercise # 5

Fig. 7: Exercise # 6

8. Support the toes on a low curbing or on a bar on the ground *not more than one inch high*. With the heels on the ground, lightly flex the knees and waist with the arms extended forward, taking up a position as though you were mounted on the horse. This will aid in a relaxed articulation of the ankle and help to place the location of the foot in the stirrup (fig. 9).

9. Rotation of the wrists forward and backward, moving them to both sides. One can commence with the arms laterally and little by little bring them to the rib cage, at the same time flexing the knees to take up the position as though mounted

with reins held in each hand. This exercise will lend softness to the articulation of the wrists (fig. 10).

10. Extension and flexion of the fingers. With the fingers lightly opened but relaxed, open and close the hand but not completely. As in the previous exercise, start with arms open and slowly bring them to the rib cage. This will serve to put looseness into the fingers (fig. 11).

11. Walk on the inside border of the feet, raising the outside border of both feet and taking the position that one would have if mounted on the horse. Go forward supported only by

Fig. 8: Exercise # 7   *Fig. 9: Exercise # 8*

Fig. 10: Exercise # 9

Fig. 11: Exercise # 10   *Fig. 12: Exercise # 11*

the inside border of the feet. This exercise will not only give flexibility to the ankle but encourage the *eversion* of the foot from the ankle down (fig. 12).

III

Leading the Horse Mounting and Dismounting

A. LEADING WITH HALTER

Approach the horse calmly and quietly, employing no brusque movements. If he is nervous, the use of a low, modulated voice will often serve to reassure him. After untying him, take up the lead line with the right hand about four inches under the halter and the end of the line in the left hand. You should be slightly ahead of him and to his left. Walk forward firmly with the assurance that he will follow you. *Do not turn around to look at him* (fig. 13).

B. LEADING WITH BRIDLE

Take up the reins about four inches below the bit by inserting the right index finger between them. Hold buckle of reins in left hand. Proceed exactly as above.

Should the horse balk or refuse to go forward, possibly because he is afraid to pass some strange object, *do not face him and attempt to pull.* Remember that the horse has much more strength than you. Indulging in a tug of war can only result in your humiliation.

A disobedience can best be resolved by breaking up the attention span of the horse, which is easily diverted. Lead him

22

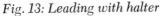

Fig. 13: Leading with halter   *Fig. 14: Leading with bridle*

firmly in a tight circle, preferably to the left since you will be on his left. The new experience of circling will divert his attention from the object threatening him and he will then very likely pass it without notice (fig. 14).

C. BRIDLING

Unfasten the large buckle of the halter, drop the noseband, but allow the halter to remain on the neck of the horse. Rebuckle the halter and allow it to remain on the neck of the horse with lead line in hand.

Unroll the reins from the bridle and insert your left arm between them. With crown-piece in right hand raise bridle to height of horse's forehead, passing muzzle of horse inside noseband. With left hand insert bit into horse's mouth. If it is necessary, introduce your thumb into the bars of the horse's jaw. With both hands pass the crown-piece behind the ears and adjust buckle and noseband. Check adjustment of bit by lengthening or shortening cheek-pieces. The bit or snaffle should be in firm contact but *neither too loose nor too tight*. In the case

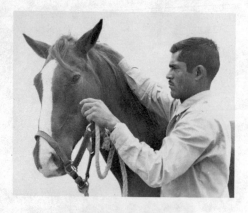

Fig. 15: Bridling

of the hunting or jumping snaffle, there should be a light contact with the corner of the lip, but *not enough to cause obvious wrinkles.*

Unbuckle and remove halter (fig. 15).

D. SADDLING

Lift and locate saddle with saddle pad, using right hand at cantle, left hand at pommel, and standing on near side of the horse. Lower saddle to back of horse with pommel at withers. Begin by placing it farther forward than normal and sliding it backward until it is properly placed. This will insure that the hair growth of the horse will be flat.

Pass to the off side (always *in front* of the horse) and buckle cinch and lower right stirrup. Pass to the near side, buckle and tighten cinch. Lower left stirrup (fig. 16).

E. ADJUSTING LENGTH OF STIRRUP LEATHERS

Proper length of stirrup leathers is of fundamental importance to the proper seat of the mounted rider. Correctly adjusted stirrups lend the rider a cushioned support for the elastic use of the ankle whether jumping or on the flat.

An *approximate* stirrup length may be obtained before mounting, as follows: Face flank of horse on near side even with stirrup leather. With straight right arm rest finger tips of right hand on saddle flap just above safety bar. Take up stirrup with left hand and extend leather until base of stirrup touches right armpit. Shorten or lengthen accordingly and adjust stirrup on off side to same length.

Since human proportions vary with individuals, the *exact* stirrup length is best adjusted after one is mounted. The following comments may serve as a guide to exact length.

The general concept of the "balance seat" should permit three stirrup lengths, depending on the work being performed.

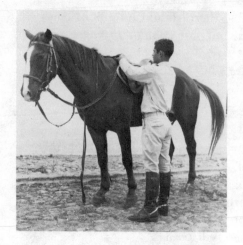

Fig. 16: Saddling

Seated on the horse, relax the legs naturally. When the base of the stirrup bangs at the anklebone, this length should be suitable for equestrian sport such as hunting or cross-country. For dressage work in the ring the stirrup should bang one hole *below* the anklebone. For high stadium jumping the stirrup should bang one hole *above* the anklebone. The latter is not necessary for low practice jumping (fig. 17).

Fig. 17: Stirrup length

F. MOUNTING AND DISMOUNTING

Stand on the near side of the horse at the point of the shoulder, facing rear. Take up the reins with the right hand at the buckle. With left index finger between, grasp reins with left hand lower down at height of mane, maintaining contact with horse's mouth. Fix left hand in mane of horse at ridge of neck.

Place left foot in stirrup, which is supported by right hand. Grip cantle of saddle with right hand. Give yourself impulse by taking a short hop with the right foot, aiding your lift with the right hand, and lift yourself in the left stirrup. Extend the right leg *straight*, well above the haunch, swing over, and settle *softly* in the saddle. Take up the right stirrup (fig. 18).

To dismount disengage the right foot. Bring right hand in front of right leg and support yourself on rear border of saddle. Swing right leg over *straight* without touching haunch. Disengage left foot and drop lightly to the ground on the toes of

Fig. 18: Mounting

both feet. *Under no circumstances should one attempt to ground right foot without first disengaging left from stirrup!* (fig. 19).

During the entire process of mounting, the well-schooled horse should stand quietly without either dancing or moving forward or backward. (See Chapter X for correction of vices.)

It will be helpful to adopt a consistent signal advising the horse that you are about to mount. This may be the slapping of the stirrup leather on the near side. It should be accompanied by the verbal command to "stand!"

Once one is seated, the horse should not move off until so commanded by the leg aids.

Fig. 19: Dismounting

In the foregoing instructions it is advised that the rider mount facing toward rear of horse. The possibility of the horse indulging in motion during mounting should always be considered. This may even occur in the well-schooled horse if he is startled by something unexpected. The majority of horses schooled to the forward impulse will move forward under these circumstances and thus assist mounting of the rider facing rear. For the occasional horse who has demonstrated a predilection for moving *backward*, the rider should mount facing *forward*. Again, the motion of the horse will assist rather than impede the mounting process.

It has been firm custom during our own period of history to mount from the near side. It is worth noting that this custom is dictated by tradition rather than practical considerations. During the period when men wore the long sword on the left side, it was obviously impractical to mount from the off side, since the sword interfered with the swinging of the left leg. At an earlier period of history, before the stirrup came into general use, most mounting was done from the off side. Most armed riders carried lances. Some distance up from the base of the lance was a leather loop. The horseman planted the lance with the right hand, placed the right foot in the loop, and vaulted up from the off side.

A well-schooled horse should be willing to accept your mounting from either side. Indeed, there are circumstances under which mounting from the off side would be preferable. During a hunt, when hounds are chasing, a rider may be either dehorsed or for one reason or another may have to dismount quickly. Remounting rapidly is essential if one is not to be left far behind. Should the horse be found on sloping ground and the high side is the off side, then certainly mounting from the off side is indicated. The near side would leave us the choice of either turning the horse around with the ensuing loss of time, or coping with the difficulty of mounting from the low and near side.

IV

Psychological and Physical Characteristics of the Horse

A. HISTORICAL EVOLUTION

Schooling the horse and riding him with any degree of success requires more than a little understanding of his capabilities, responses, and reactions. A knowledge of how he differs from other species will be found most useful. Therefore, it is worthwhile inquiring into his origins and even comparing them with our own, since we, like the horse, are the product of evolution.

If we understand man to be distinguished by the "big brain," then our entire history can be compressed into some half million years. The primates of the preceding half million years had evidently developed the opposable thumb, and leaving the shelter of the trees, had even developed carnivorous appetites. We still cannot properly regard them as men.

The history of the horse encompasses some sixty to seventy million years. Eohippus, sometimes referred to as the "dawn horse," made the scene in the Eocene era. He was a little larger than a cocker spaniel, had articulated toes, and his evolution seems to have been directed to a life in the swamps. From then on paleontology has successfully reconstructed his evolutionary pattern. We have not successfully explained either his migra-

tions or his various disappearances and reappearances in the
Western Hemisphere.

Comparing our own brief history to that of the horse, it is
reasonable to suppose that in some sixty million years of
evolution the horse has developed faculties that we either
have never possessed, or if we ever did possess them, we have
forgotten them on our way to a different and accelerated
evolutionary process. These faculties, which we lack, the horse
demonstrates daily. We will discuss them in more detail later.

One question often asked of me is, "Is the horse intelligent?"
Another is, "Is the horse more intelligent than the dog or cat,
or elephant?" Such questions are most difficult to answer unless
we first consider a definition of intelligence.

Webster precedes the full definition of intelligence with
the following:

> Faculty of understanding; capacity to know or apprehend. May
> cover *any* power of apprehension. (Italics mine.)

It is well known that the horse learns by direct *apprehension* by means of association, as distinct from the human, who
learns by cogitation and rationalization. It seems to me that
the sixty-million-year evolution of the horse itself demonstrates
an extraordinary intelligence as to what was necessary to both
survival and growth. In sixty million years Eohippus has
evolved into the modern "Equus." He has come from some
twenty-five pounds of weight to a species that weighs any-
where from a few-hundred-pound pony to a twenty-five-hun-
dred-pound draft horse. He came out of the swamps onto the
plains. His articulated toes coalesced into the hoof, making him
the "soliped" we know today. His speed enables him to evade
most dangers that threaten his life.

All this was accomplished during a period when other (and
larger) species simply died out because they could not adapt
in order to sustain themselves.

Intelligence?

I think so.

The quality of intelligence is peculiar to a given species even though the precepts may be general. In this respect the comparison of intelligence between species is largely a useless endeavor because of the generalities involved. A canine intelligence is not properly comparable to an equine one, any more than it is comparable to that of the feline. Because Fido will sit up and beg for your approval, and your horse will not, does not necessarily demonstrate superiority of the canine intelligence. It demonstrates merely a *difference*. It is true that animal psychologists have developed general tests of intelligence that largely ignore special differences. The results of these tests demonstrate that of all domestic animals the pig is by far the most intelligent. It is doubtful that because of this finding many people will be trading in their dogs for pigs. The truth is that it is often the differences in species intellect that attract us rather than the generalities present.

We as humans are terribly prone to indulge in anthropomorphic fancies concerning animal species. But the attribution of quasi-human or desired qualities is a poor indicator of inherent special intelligence. Gertrude Stein would have said, "A horse is a horse is a horse is a horse."

It would be comforting at this point to be able to tell you that scientifically we fully understand the behavioral patterns of the horse and the significance of his inherent aggressions. The truth is that we do not, except in a very general way. In the last three decades the whole science of animal behaviorism has been quite revolutionized, thanks to the tireless inquiries of such dedicated investigators as Konrad Lorenz and others like him. Previous to these developments it was generally believed that studies of the lion in the London zoo would yield valid knowledge of lion behaviorism. We now know that this was a fallacious assumption. A lion in the London Zoo no longer shares behavioral patterns with a lion in his natural environment. He is merely a neurotic prisoner. Normal human behavior patterns cannot be studied either in prisons or in asylums.

Since the 1930s, literally hundreds of species have been scientifically observed in their natural habitats, from tropical fish, birds, fowl to most species of mammal. Scientists have lived with prides of lions, Rhesus monkeys, baboons, and gorillas. Out of these observations have come the new knowledge of animal behaviorism and the concept of territorial aggression. In this particular sense, no scientist has studied the horse, and it becomes increasingly difficult to do so. Largely the horse has become completely domesticated except for a few preserved herds in North America—where the ecological balance is difficult to preserve—and possibly a few herds on the steppes of Asia.

The general facts that we *are* aware of form the following picture:

The social structure of the horse in his natural habitat is of course a patriarchy. The herd consists of mares, primarily the harem of the dominant stallion, and the younger stallions, that have not challenged the leader for dominance. The herd clusters predominantly in a circle with the mares with foals forming the center. Around them will be found the mares without foals, and the young stallions form the periphery, ready to take the brunt of any attack on the herd.

The dominant stallion seems to do most of the sentry duty. The horse, being herbivorous, is a grazing animal and his habitual position is head down into the grass. For size of body the stomach cavity is quite small, indicating that nature intends that the horse graze continuously rather than indulge, as we do, in large feedings at intervals.

The nature of equine vision gives the horse more than 180 degrees of surveillance ahead while grazing. By looking between his back legs he also commands more than 180 degrees of vision behind. This, together with extremely acute sensitivities of hearing and smell (plus the possible existence of faculties not yet understood), enables the sentry horse to sense danger at appreciable distances.

By command not yet understood he will cause the herd to

move off at the gallop. He may either drive the herd or lead, or a combination of both. When the lead stallion decides the danger is evaded, he will command the herd to halt, and all will resume grazing.

It is not the nature of the horse to stand and face danger but invariably to *run away from it*. It is true that an angry stallion can appear to be a most fearsome spectacle. However, on examination it will be seen that he possesses little of the aggressive armament of the predatory species. He can clobber with the forehand and he can bite. That is all.

It is worthy of note that when two stallions battle for supremacy they seldom battle to the death. When one has been obviously bested he will usually retire, hang his head, and wander off to start a new herd.

To return for a moment to the question of intelligence: The lore of the Old West is amply larded with stories of the romantic cowboy who longed to catch and tame "the beautiful white stallion." The cowboys who chased the elusive stallion and his herd had everything in their favor. They had hardy and trained horses. They were often skilled ropers. Nevertheless, the elusive stallion and his herd often led them on fruitless chases that lasted for weeks. So well did the stallion know the terrain and so ample were his mental resources that he was often able to hide his herd in blind canyons, let his pursuers pass, double back, and start the chase over again.

Again, we must consider an intelligence in the light of the demands for existence of a particular species.

In view of what we know about the horse, we must be intrigued with those of his qualities that permit an intimate association with man. Predominant evidence puts the domestication of the horse somewhere near 2000 B.C. There are a few writers on the subject who put the event several thousand years previous, but no firm evidence has been adduced for such an assumption. There appears, therefore, to be about four thousand years of partnership between man and the horse. In the beginning the horse was used to pull farm vehicles and war chariots, the same use as was made of his predecessor, the onager. Sometime later he was ridden. From about 2000 B.C. until the invention of the steam engine in the nineteenth century, man's land transportation was limited by the speed and endurance of the horse.

In terms of the partnership between man and the horse it is worth making the point that we ride the horse because the horse is *willing*; not because we are so devilishly clever. The zebra is an equine animal quite similar to the horse in some respects. Nobody rides zebras, simply because a zebra is not willing and will not cooperate.

The horse is a herd animal, used to seeking leadership from another horse. In his domesticated state he is evidently able to make a transference and look to a human for leadership, provided the human makes possible the assured orderliness of existence and relief from responsibility.

In effect, the horse signs a bargain. He says, "If you will assure me an orderly existence, a decent place to live, adequate food and grooming, and the exercise necessary to keep me fit, then I will do my best to learn all these silly things that seem to please you, such as complicated dressage maneuvers and jumping all these crazy obstacles." Most horses are quite faithful about keeping their part of the bargain. Alas! Some humans are not!

B. PSYCHOLOGY

One of the several faculties making possible the schooling of the horse is the imitative one. A green horse working in an arena in line with schooled horses quickly begins to imitate the patterns of motion of the other horses and thus hastens his learning period. Imitatively, the horse also takes both courage and fright from another horse or horses. He will much more readily go over an obstacle when another horse has immediately preceded him over it; conversely, when horses are closely following in a hunt and one horse refuses a fence, it is quite likely that the next horse will refuse, and these refusals may well go on far down the line.

Closely allied to the imitative faculty is the herd-bound instinct of the horse, sometimes referred to as "magnetism." He seems to find security in the presence of his kind. He would much rather work in the company of other horses than alone. Almost no horses are "loners." There is hardly any equine equivalent of the human recluse. This in spite of the fact that aggression within the species is often demonstrated by both kicking and biting.

1. Memory

In terms of schooling, by far the most valuable equine trait we have to work with is memory. The horse possesses an almost infallible and long-lasting memory. He learns rapidly and seldom forgets an impressive experience. In this respect his memory for experience is far superior to that of most humans.

2. Faculty of Forming Habits

We said previously that the horse apparently learns by direct apprehension rather than by intelligent rationalization. It is now time to add that this direct apprehension is dependent on associated phenomena.

It has long been observed in cavalry regiments that the remount horse learns the meaning of the various bugle calls much more rapidly than does the human recruit. While the green soldier is still struggling to sort out one bugle call from another *intellectually*, the horse has already learned them by direct apprehension and *association* with the time of day and the activity being performed.

Furthermore, if one blows a given call on a bugle at a fixed hour and lines a group of horses up in a given order to be groomed, fed, and watered, and this process is repeated for a few days, then after only three or four experiences the horses will respond to the bugle by lining themselves up in the same order and awaiting a pleasant reward. This is often more than is expected of the human recruit after a similar brief experience.

There are innumerable stories to illustrate the remarkable persistence of the equine memory. I should like to offer one out of my own experience. It will be found that most horses, if stabled in a group for even a short time, will make no effort to escape should they find themselves loose. This, too, is probably due to the herd-bound instinct. There are, however, notable exceptions. I had one horse who, whenever he found himself loose, would invariably take off for the hills. He was usually soon caught and brought back by my staff. On one occasion, however, his absence was not noted for some time. This happened eight years after I had bought the horse from a ranch some twenty miles distant.

A full day's search failed to turn up the horse, nor did a second day's search. On the third day, when my men were saddling up to hunt again, I told them not to bother, that I was quite sure the horse had gone back to his home ranch. Since he had not seen his home ranch in eight years, they questioned my sanity.

I drove my car to his original ranch and found him in the fields outside the corral. Judging by the distance, he must have headed straight across country and traveled steadily to get there.

The predilection of the horse for forming habits is of course dependent on his memory factor. There is a saying that if a horse does something three times he has formed a lifelong habit. This is largely true. In schooling this represents a double-edged sword. Desirable habits are relatively easily impressed, but *so are undesirable habits*. Make every effort to prevent repetition of vices or bad habits!

The education of a horse is a rather Pavlovian process based upon *consistency* and constant repetition. The associated stimuli, whether vocal or physical aid, must always be given or applied in the same way if repetition by association is to prove of value. What we are here attempting is the final transformation of *conscious* association into *subconscious* association by repetition. If this process is guided by a proper concept of reward and punishment, it will produce successive strata in the impressionable memory centers. New reflexes will be formed until the response to a given signal is automatic.

For satisfactory performance of the horse it is desirable that response be both *predictable* and *rapid*. Both these factors demand *automatic* response. Predictability insures, for example, that given the leg aids to go forward, the horse will not go backward; that he will *stop* when the aids to the halt are applied. Rapidity insures that he will yield response at the instant it is demanded, not later. Under certain circumstances both horse and rider may be subject to a certain amount of danger. Averting that danger will depend greatly on both predictability and rapidity of the horse's responses, assuming of course that the rider is able to command capably. The rider who waits for his horse to get him out of trouble is in a poor position indeed.

So far we have spoken only of repetition, since this is the means of usual progress in the horse's development. It should be noted, however, that under certain circumstances *intensity* of one associated impression can be substituted for repetition and thus reduce schooling time. Appropriate examples that come to mind involve both fire and water. Some horses will object to jumping a water obstacle. Should this be the case, an intense original impression must be made to convince the horse that his fears are groundless. He can be *led* through the water for instance. But finally he must jump it. Should he object, the rider must of course intensify the impressor aids and be assisted by a trainer with longe whip, applying same vigorously under the hocks at the instant of indicated takeoff. The same thing is true of a fire obstacle except that obviously the horse cannot be led through the latter. He must be *impulsed* through. In all the foregoing we are substituting intensity of impression for repetition.

Since several references have been made to the precepts

of reward and punishment, it will be useful to define these terms. They do not imply the extremes of feeding the horse carrots or beating him with a stick. Many things can constitute both reward and punishment. The tone of the voice is one. A pat on the neck and a few words of praise constitute a reward and are so accepted by the horse. He doesn't have to understand the words. He knows by the *tone* of your voice that you approve of him. He will also be humiliated by a tone of *disapproval*, accompanied by the same slap, and accept it as a punishment. Severity of punishment implies the use of the crop, accompanied by a voice of strong disapproval.

It is well to remember that horses have a keen sense of justice. They are inclined to accept deserved punishment. But a spirited horse will rebel strongly against an unjust punishment. Before indulging in any form of punishment, the rider should be absolutely sure that the horse understood what was wanted and deliberately rebelled. It is worthwhile to ask yourself, "Was it my fault? Did I confuse the horse?"

Never punish a horse to indulge your own bad temper. He will lose confidence in you.

Never punish a horse because you have forced him to concentrate on a difficult task beyond the period of his normal attention-span.

The normal attention-span of a colt or filly is limited, as is that of children. If forced to concentrate for a longer period than they are capable of, they will become frustrated and recalcitrant. Any sensitive observer should know when this limit has been reached. The horse will proceed more satisfactorily by encouragement than by discouragement. If your young horse seems to find difficulty learning a given exercise, do not continue to the point of discouragement and put him up feeling like a failure. Your next day's work will be more difficult. Go back to an exercise he does know how to do so that you can justly praise him. Send him to the barn feeling like a success.

Treat him much as you would your own child, whom you

also expect to learn difficult skills, with firmness, kindness, and love. He is terribly dependent on you. *Your love will be rewarded.*

3.   The Effect of Psychology on Motion

We have said previously that for sixty million years the horse has survived by running away from danger. We have come to recognize this fact as the basis of "forward motion." Every horse has a built-in knowledge that it is thus his race has survived. The process of schooling consists in part of converting uncontrolled motion into controlled motion, subject to command of the aids. However, during the schooling period one *should not discourage the natural forward impulse of the horse.* Under these discouragements I would include hard-pulling hands of the rider, use of the crop on the forehand, and *any or all harsh or cruel bits.*

No amount of schooling will ever erase sixty million years of racial memory. The best-schooled horse, if sufficiently frightened or frustrated, may "run away." This should be regarded as a normal reaction of a horse who has momentarily reached the limit of his psychological tolerance. It need not necessarily characterize a dangerous horse or a "rebel." Genuine "rebels" among horses, as far as my own experience indicates, are in a far greater minority than human rebels. Most "rebels" are the product of mistreatment and can be rehabilitated merely by restoration of their shaken confidence in human beings.

4.   Confidence of the Horse in the Rider

It is impossible to deal intimately with horses over a period of years without coming to realize that their ability to divine human character is rather awesome. It is again a sense perception in the horse that we cannot pin down on the basis of present knowledge, but its existence is not subject to doubt.

I shall here go out on a limb and state categorically that the majority of horses, at the moment the strange rider puts the leg over and settles down in the saddle, make an instant appraisal of both the rider's character and riding ability, and they are seldom wrong.

It is constantly demonstrated in a school such as ours, where the horses rest on Sundays. At best, Monday mornings they are feeling frisky. Should it happen that the weather is cold and windy, they will be even friskier. Often it is necessary for the staff to longe or ride the more energetic horses Monday mornings in order to take off some of their top energy before green riders mount up.

Let us assume, as has been demonstrated many times, that in spite of this procedure a frisky horse unseats a few green riders. This will not be due to meanness but purely to good spirits. However, make no mistake. If a horse unseats you, he is inclined to feel rather proud of himself. Many horses who have just unseated a rider will take off at the collected trot, their tails held high, demonstrating to the other horses that they have just successfully unseated an unfortunate rider. On the other hand, a horse who tries to buck you off and does not succeed feels humiliated. It has happened on several occasions that on these active Monday mornings we have had a visiting fireman or professional horseman totally unknown to the horses. After the horse in question has bucked off several green riders, the professional rider requests my permission to try.

He mounts up, swings the leg over, and the horse stands like a statue. Why?

It would seem obvious that at this instant the horse makes two appraisals of the rider: (1) "This person knows how to ride. If I try to buck him off, he will just sit there and I will be humiliated in front of all my friends." (2) "This person has a strong character. If I try to buck him off he will give me hell! He may even use that nasty crop! I am just going to stand here and demonstrate my respect for him."

We can easily conclude therefore that much of the quality of the performance of the horse will depend on his regard for the rider in terms of both ability and character. Under certain circumstances the rider asks the horse to abdicate his own judgment in favor of that of the rider. If the horse respects the rider in terms of the two factors stated above, he will so abdicate. If he does not, he will have doubts. If you come to a ravine in the country and ask your horse to jump it, you must convince him of both your superior equestrian judgment and your superior determination. He would just as soon find an easier way around the ravine. Once convinced of your superiority he will relinquish his judgment to yours and make the attempt, borrowing courage, as it were, from your assurance.

Never come into any obstacle with doubt in your mind, depending on the courage of the horse to take you over. The horse will instantly sense your fear and lose heart!

C. PHYSICAL CHARACTERISTICS

1. Anterior, Middle, and Posterior

For purposes of analysis of function we may divide the horse into three parts: the anterior, the middle, and the posterior.

The anterior serves for both direction and balance. The neck of the horse is sometimes referred to as "the balancer." The head, which may weigh some twenty-four pounds, serves as a pendulum at the end of the neck. The horse therefore, uses the head and neck much as we use our arms as a counterbalance. As we swing our arms while walking, the horse extends and retracts the head and neck. The more extended the walk, the more horizontal displacement will occur. When we are in danger of falling, we throw out our arms. The horse in danger of falling throws the head and neck in order to maintain his balance. The fallen horse attempting to rise must move the head and neck first, then rise on the forehand, and lastly on the hinds. When you are treating an injured horse that is lying upon the ground, it will accomplish little to hold down his quarters. However, one capable person can hold the head down and the horse is unable to rise.

The middle of the horse represents the area of least displacement at all three gaits. Each gait results in a different type of displacement to which the rider must accommodate.

The posterior of the horse represents essentially his motive power in both forward motion and jumping.

The horse possesses the faculty of physically lengthening or shortening his body, and these extremes are referred to as extension and collection. The center of gravity of the extended horse will be found to be over the fourteenth vertebrate (approximately the highest point of the withers). As the horse collects, this center of gravity will move progressively back to the fifteenth, sixteenth, and finally the seventeenth vertebrate. During the process of collection, the horse's neck is raised and arched, and his haunches and hocks are brought under him, increasing both power and elasticity.

Collection implies that the base of support (which is determined by the rectangle connecting the four supporting members) is *smaller* than the mass above it. Extension implies that the base of support is *larger* than the mass above it. The disunited or uncollected horse has relatively little facility either for complicated dressage figures or for jumping.

2. Blood Circulation

The horse suffers from a general vulnerability of the legs which is due to inequality of blood circulation; one main artery feeds each limb. The blood circulation of the legs is generally poor until the horse has been put to strong exercise. This factor results in several peculiarities.

Since healing of injuries depends largely on blood circulation, leg cuts or injuries heal much more slowly than cuts or injuries to another part of the body. Every effort should be made, therefore, to protect the legs of the horse both in work and in shipping.

The same circulatory deficiency demands that the horse be warmed up slowly and cooled out slowly. When he comes out of the barn "cold" because of poor blood circulation in the legs, there will be relatively little spring in his gait. The articulation of the pastern normally cushions the shock of each print of the gait. When the horse is "cold" the pastern is stiff and poorly articulated, and the rider will feel the jolt of each print.

It is essential that the cold horse be warmed up progressively. This indicates at least seven or eight minutes at the walk, an equal time at the trot, and at least a few minutes at the canter. *Only then will the horse be physically fit for strenuous work.*

Once the horse has worked strenuously, *he should not be allowed to stand still for any length of time.* Since the blood of the legs is now circulating rapidly, no difficulty is encountered as long as the horse is in action. If the hot horse is held inactive a serum is often exuded through the arterial wall resulting in small soft swellings on the pastern known as wind galls. These are often transient. Should they become hard and permanent, they can inhibit the horse's performance.

The hot horse when finished working should be walked until he is absolutely dry. *He should never be put up until properly cooled out.* The tack should not be removed before he is cooled out unless it is to be replaced with a stable sheet. The kidneys of the horse are close to the surface of his back. Should a cold wind sweep over his back when he is highly sweated, he can easily contract pneumonia. The girth should be loosened and some air allowed under the saddle while he is being cooled out.

The normal body temperature of the horse is 100.3°F. By sweating, the horse is able to throw off excess heat and stabilize body temperature.

D. SENSES

1. Vision (Distinctive Characteristics)

Much of what a horse does can be understood in terms of his vision. Even a casual observation of the lateral placement of his eyes indicates that he sees a very different world than do we who have frontality of vision. Incidentally, there is a theory that attempts to relate frontality of vision to level of intelligence simply because it is a primate characteristic. This theory would suggest that a Pekingese has a higher level of intelligence than a shepherd or collie, which is hardly the case.

The triangulation of frontally placed eyes is extremely short. (By triangulation I refer to that point at which binocularity begins or ceases. Within that triangulation two images are transmitted to the brain without depth perception.) The triangulation of laterally placed eyes is extremely long. This is further complicated in the horse by a broad frontal blind area.

If you put your finger close to your nose and close the left eye, your finger will appear to have a fixed position. Now if you simultaneously open the left eye and close the right eye, your finger will appear to have jumped a considerable distance to the right. Since our triangulation is so short, this phenomenon rarely bothers us, but it is constantly happening to the horse. The leaf floating in the breeze appears to us to have consistent motion. If it passes two feet in front of the horse, it jumps from the vision of one eye to the other, and the horse shies off it (fig. 20).

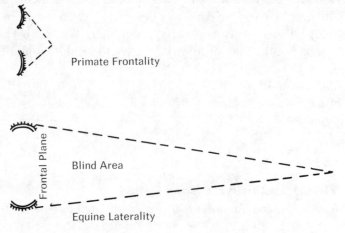

Fig. 20: Triangulation of vision, human-equine

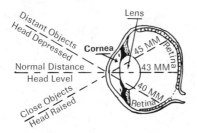

Fig. 21: Section of the eye of the horse

The normal point of vision of the horse seems to be distance unless he has reason to concentrate on a closer object. When he does make this change it seems to take longer for the close image to resolve than it would, for instance, for us. There appear to be several reasons for this.

Most animals, including man, fish, and reptiles, focus vision by altering the shape of the lens (placing it nearer or farther from the cornea) by virtue of the ciliary muscle. While the horse has the ciliary muscle, it appears to be relatively inactive, resulting in little change of shape of the lens. Another difference is that the retina of the human eye is consistently concave. The horse has a "ramped" retina which may be as much as five mm closer to the cornea at the lower part than the upper (fig. 21).

The result of these difficulties is that the horse must move the head in order both to change point of view and also to find the optimum position to achieve sharp focus. As a rule he will raise his head to see close objects and lower it for distant vision. Indications are that his vision is somewhat astigmatic.

A horse coming in to an obstacle should be given enough freedom of head movement to keep the obstacle in focus.

It is well worth remembering that a *horse at the point of takeoff can no longer see the portion of the obstacle he has to jump.* The average point of takeoff is four feet from the bar. At this distance the center of the bar has already entered his frontal blind area. He must *remember* its exact height in order to clear it. By turning his head he can see only the left and right extremes. The horse does not merely launch himself high and hope for the best. He *calculates* height carefully. The clever jumper clears the bar at minimum. He does not waste his energy in useless height.

The peripheral vision of the horse is naturally quite different from our own. He sees a broad arc to either side and *to the rear*. At will he is able to keep the right hand and right leg of the rider under observation as well as the other side. It is this peripheral visual ability that enables him to *anticipate* the action of the leg and respond before it has actually touched him.

Position of the ears is often a sound indication of where the horse is directing his visual attention. The horse approaching the fence with both ears pricked forward is obviously giving it the attention of both eyes. If the right ear pricks forward and the left one back, he may well be worried about something the rider is doing on the left side. Both ears laid back often indicates recalcitrance or an unwillingness to jump.

A horse does not back into a wall unknowingly, because he *sees* it.

The question of the horse's ability to see color has long been debated. By far the majority of animal physiologists are convinced that the horse cannot *see* color and that the dog is similarly color-blind. Since no final proof for this has been adduced, to my knowledge, I am inclined to regard it still as hypothesis only. The evidence advanced to support the belief that the horse cannot see color is primarily based on the structure of the retina. It is believed that color vision is only made possible by a cone-rich retina and a well developed occipital lobe. Horses seem to have a rod-rich retinal structure rather than cone-rich. Because of this structural condition it would seem that the nerve system is inadequate for the transmission of color vision.

This may well prove to be the case. At the same time it should again be emphasized that the actual scientific research extant (specific to the horse) is inadequate to justify final conclusions. Again, here we are so far proceeding on a subjective assumptive base calculated by known faculties of man and the higher primates.

The seeing of color is a subjective process. There is no way of describing a given color to someone who has been born blind. Nor do all people see color in the same hues. Color-blindness often occurs among human males. (Much less often in the human female.) Extent and type of insensitivity varies with the individual among the color-blind.

My personal experience leads me to the conviction that horses can *distinguish* one color from another, whatever the subjective process involved. Some horses are afraid of red trucks but green trucks do not bother them. If a horse crashes badly into a red and white fence, there will be difficulty getting him over another red and white fence—but he will go willingly over a blue and white fence.

This leaves the phenomenon of *seeing* color in the realm of scientific controversy, where it still properly belongs.

I will also advance the firm belief that with no trouble at all a horse can distinguish texture indicating basic material. In a show ring it is the custom to paint some obstacles to represent stone walls. This may divert the public but it does not fool the horse. A painted stone wall can be knocked down, and he knows it. When you take him over an actual stone wall he carefully lends it the respect its fixed nature demands.

The night vision of the horse appears to be considerably superior to our own, even though the transition from light to dark requires more time of adjustment for the equine vision than for human.

On one occasion in Spain I found myself on a three-hour night ride in rather dangerous country. There was no moon whatever. At times none of the riders could distinguish the footing. By their willingness to trot, the horses demonstrated that they could easily distinguish the footing. On other occasions, when the horses were caught in the total blackness of a ravine, for instance, no urging would produce more than a cautious walk, indicating that even they were having difficulty making out the footing.

2. Hearing

Normal equine sense of hearing seems to be extremely acute. The human audible range is from 20 to 20,000 cycles. Dogs have an audible range up to 100,000. Again, less scientific work has been done in this field on horses than on dogs. It is still obvious that the horse has a cyclic range far exceeding ours.

The horse seems to hear over distances impossible to human hearing. It often happens that a hunt may be in progress a few miles distant. The humans in the stable can hear not a sound of hooves, hounds, or horn. Often the experienced hunter in stall will become agitated and break out in a sweat of excitement.

It may well be that the actual auditory sense of the horse is augmented by ground vibrations that are conducted through the bones of the limbs to the skull and registered by the middle ear.

Although loud noises may startle horses, soft sounds seem to be more meaningful to them. It is not difficult to condition horses to gunfire. Cavalry horses quickly become inured to it and will charge into it on command. They will also be still on their sides while the trooper rests his carbine on them and fires steadily. But the horse that ignores gunfire may be frightened out of his wits by the rattling of paper at his ear. Undoubtedly, during their long evolution, the soft sounds of a predator rustling leaves represented considerably more danger than a loud clap of thunder. Should you wish to secure the interest and confidence of a strange horse, you will accomplish it best by whispering to him and stoking him as gently as you would a bird.

In the mid-nineteenth century John Solomon Rarey became world famous for the ability to dominate completely any "rebel" horse within half an hour. He did this by the use of a hitch of his own devising that caused the horse finally to go down and lie on its side. Then he dominated the horse by "whispering" to him. Obviously a form of oral hypnotism was involved.

In England particularly it is the habit of elderly grooms of the old school constantly to hiss through their teeth as they brush and groom the horse, reassuring him and keeping him calm.

3.   Olfactory Sense

This sense, too, is acutely developed in the horse. A stallion can smell a mare in heat over surprising distances. It should be noted that a horse does almost all breathing through the nasal passages and almost none through the mouth, which is limited by the soft palate. The nostrils of a horse are one of his most expressive characteristics and indeed can indicate many of his emotional reactions. The smell of smoke and flames is particularly distasteful and frightening to the horse, but nevertheless it is not too difficult to teach a horse to jump fire obstacles.

Obviously the sense of smell serves to satisfy much of the curiosity of the horse. He will sniff at people, food, and strange objects in order to identify them. A new obstacle on your field offers less fright to the horse if he has been allowed a previous opportunity to sniff at it.

4.   Proprioceptive Sense

A keen equine attribute and absolutely essential to his locomotion is the sense in humans that gives us absolute knowledge of the location of the members of our body even in total darkness. The horse in action must have an absolute and accurate knowledge of the placement of his hind legs at any given moment. There are jumpers who clear fences closely by at the last moment twisting the haunch so that the hinds go over at an angle to the bar rather than parallel to it. It is the proprioceptive sense that enables them to gauge accurately the amount of torque necessary to clear. Many foals are able to canter one hour after birth, indicating already a fully functioning proprioceptive sense.

5. Extrasensory Perception

The whole area of equine ESP is of course as controversial as is the same phenomenon in humans, but with one signal difference. *The average horse demonstrates much more extrasensory perception than does the average human.* What is most difficult to determine is exactly where a heightened but known sense leaves off and an unknown perception takes over. If we go back to the hunter in stall who demonstrates by his actions that he knows a distant hunt is in progress, inaudible to humans, we must either assume a sense of hearing hardly credible, even if assisted by ground vibrations, or the functioning of a yet unidentified sense. Even if we assume the former, the many known examples of both the horse's concurrent knowledge and his *foreknowledge* cannot all be explained on these grounds.

It is my own experience and that of many other horsemen that over a long association between a particular horse and one rider, the horse will finally begin completely to anticipate the aids. It must be admitted that the horse is a keen observer of even slight visual phenomena that escape human attention. Even the highly sophisticated rider who has achieved independence of the aids by reducing his reflex actions to a minimum may indulge in slight reflexive idiosyncrasies of which he is unaware. Some people, when putting a cigarette into the right side of the mouth, automatically narrow the left eye. It is to this type of subtle reflex that we are referring. Since we know the horse to be such a keen observer of subtleties, we may assume that he finally responds to these small associated and often preliminary phenomena without awaiting the aid itself. But again, not all the horse's concurrent knowledge and foreknowledge can be explained on these grounds. There is an old saying among horsemen, "Think hard to the left and your horse will go to the left." There is a lot of truth in this saying.

Charles Darwin was one of the first to note that when we wish an object to move in a certain direction, there is an unconscious *involuntary* movement in that direction termed motor automatism or ideomotor behavior.

Personally I am quite convinced of the fact that certain sensitive horses, after long experience with one rider, are able to apprehend his intentions without the aids. I will go even further. I believe, based on firsthand experience, that certain horses under the above circumstances develop a *predictive* faculty. They are able to predict the intention of the rider before he himself is conscious of coming to a decision.

Recently, while I was lecturing on this subject in the Escuela, a woman rider who experienced one of Peru's worst earthquakes told me the following: She was at the riding club, in the company of many other riders, when all the horses seemed to go mad. Almost every rider was thrown. The frenzy lasted two and a half minutes. While some riders were still picking themselves up and others were attempting to catch their horses, the earthquake struck. There had previously been no sound audible to the riders.

As a final example we can cite the homing instinct of horses. Even if we allow that it may often be assisted by the known senses, there is still no discovered physical center for this sense. You may take a horse by a circuitous route far across country. If you give him his head to return to his stable, he will not return by the roundabout way you have come but directly by the shortest route. When he encounters impossible barriers he may retrace and find his way around them but he will try constantly to maintain the most direct route possible. His progress will be facilitated if he is upwind from his stables, and this obviously points to assistance by his olfactory sense. However, even if he is downwind, he will still find his way home in day, fog, or the darkness of night.

V

The Seat of the Mounted Rider

A. THE CONCEPT OF THE "BALANCE" SEAT

The seat employed at the Escuela is based upon the concept of the "balance" seat as generally practiced in international riding. Although there are national differences of emphasis, the general precepts employed are fairly consistent. It was adopted as official seat by the U.S. Cavalry as early as 1922 and was analyzed in detail in *Horsemanship and Horsemastership*, published by the Academic Division of the Cavalry School, Fort Riley, Kansas, in 1942. This was, sadly enough, just prior to the complete mechanization of all U.S. Cavalry.

The balance seat, as we practice it, really consists of three seats or three positions (fig. 22). They may be defined as the deep seat, light seat, and forward seat, and their use will depend on the kind of equestrian work being done. Type of work being done will also permit three different stirrup lengths, as previously explained under "Mounting."

The "deep seat" is most suitable for dressage and for most (but not all) work done in the arena. The "light seat" is indicated for the hand gallop in the exterior and is useful in polo and the hunting field. The "forward seat" implies a desire on the part of the rider to send the horse "flat out" and make the most speed possible. This might be desirable in the hunt when hounds are in cry or in a cross-country trial against the clock.

54

Fig. 22:
Deep seat

Light seat

Forward seat

Please note that in the "light seat" the rider has displaced forward at the waist but is still *sitting*. In the "forward seat" the rider has displaced even further forward but now all the weight is in the stirrups and the seat is actually out of the saddle. This position takes considerable weight off the back of the horse.

It is our firm belief that the "forward seat" should *not* be maintained when approaching a fence, even though one notes that this is often done in hunting circles in the United States, Canada, and England. The forward seat implies that the horse is going not only fast but extended. The predominant weight will be on his forehand. The uncollected horse has much less power to jump than the collected horse. If your horse has had the proper training in basic dressage, he will shorten stride and "come back to you" at the instant that you sit. He will then be able to launch himself over the fence with his haunches and hocks under him instead of dragging them along behind him.

In various countries of Europe I have ridden "cross-country horses" who had been taught no collection whatsoever. They had plenty of forward impulse but knew nothing else. I find such horses most unsatisfying to ride. It becomes practically impossible to sit the canter. There is no alternative but to go forward and "go with the horse" and let the poor fellow do the best he can on the fences. There are breeds of horses who seem to possess more natural collection than others, even if unschooled. I recall riding a large Andalusian stallion in Spain. He had been taught neither basic dressage nor jumping. Aside from his inability to jump, I found him a most pleasant horse to ride. His natural collection gave quick response to any change in the rider's seat. From an extended gallop he would come in instantly to a collected seated canter. A horse of such natural facility can be a great joy both to school and ride.

In terms of the mounted rider we divide the body into three parts. From the waist to the top of the head the body must be free to displace forward, slightly backward, and laterally in order both to preserve equilibrium and to influence the

Fig. 23: Balance seat

horse. From the knee joint to the foot the leg must be mobile in order to impulse and influence the horse. We regard the portion from the knee to the waist as the "fixed seat." This part "goes with" the horse.

In terms of maintenance of equilibrium, the best example that comes to mind is a plate of conically shaped gelatin. If we shake the plate backward and forward and take pictures, we find that the top of the gelatin displaces backward and forward. If shaken from side to side, the gelatin responds laterally. In other words, the gelatin changes its center of gravity in response to external motion in order to preserve equilibrium and stay on the plate. This is essentially what the rider does. If the upper body does not move to maintain equilibrium, the base of support will shift and the rider may go off his horse.

The "balance" seat is so termed because it puts the rider in balance in relation to his own center of gravity. When this seat is properly employed there is no need to squeeze inordinately

with either the inner thighs or the knees, as there is if the
rider moves behind his own center of gravity. It is "balance"
that keeps the rider on, not pressure.

Fig. 23 demonstrates the deep phase of the balance seat.
A vertical line dropped from the mastoid of the ear should fall
approximately through the anklebone. This line represents
both the rider's vertical axis and his center of gravity in this
position. The weight of the upper body is balanced over its
base of support. This implies that the leg must be flexed at
the knee and carried *back of the girth*.

If you wish to check both the position of your lower leg and
your ankle flexion, there is a very simple proof: Rise in the
stirrups and maintain yourself at both the walk and trot, with
back concave and shoulders open, looking straight ahead. If
your lower leg is far enough back and your ankle sufficiently
flexed, you will have no difficulty maintaining balance in this
position. If you fall backward to the saddle, *your lower leg is
too far forward* and *your ankle insufficiently flexed*. You are
therefore behind your center of gravity and unable to accompany the horse.

The rider has to be concerned not only with his own center
of gravity but with the constantly shifting center of gravity of
the horse. Fig. 24 shows the center of gravity of the extended
horse located at the fourteenth vertabra. This center will
change as the horse shortens or lengthens stride. The two centers of gravity may be thought of as two lines in a range-finder.
The rider should strive at all times to keep his center of gravity
as close to that of the horse as possible. The range of forward
displacement from the vertical to the forward seat enables the
rider not only to go *with* the horse but to *influence* him to extend or collect.

Collection, incidentally, is not primarily achieved by the
hands, even in a double bridle where the rider has the leverage
of the curb at his disposal. To attempt to achieve this by the
hand, in double bridle, will usually result in mere overflexion
of the neck, rather than true collection. Initially, collection is

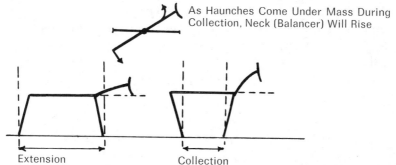

As Haunches Come Under Mass During
Collection, Neck (Balancer) Will Rise

Extension   Collection
Base of Support Larger Than Mass • Base of Support Smaller Than Mass

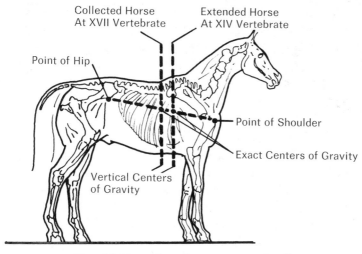

Collected Horse   Extended Horse
At XVII Vertebrate   At XIV Vertebrate

Point of Hip

Point of Shoulder

Exact Centers of Gravity

Vertical Centers
of Gravity

Fig. 24: Extremes of extension and collection

achieved by the deep seat and the application of the legs
behind the girth. The horse responds by lifting the neck. He
should confidently *seek* the snaffle in order to encounter the
support of the rider's hand. As his neck arches, his haunches
should come under his mass and the profile of his head approach
the vertical. The rider should take rein as it is thus yielded and
keep it on light contact of the hand.

The neck of the horse is often referred to as the "balancer."

At all gaits a certain freedom of movement of the neck is required for the normal forward progress of the horse. Schooling requires freedom of *extension* in order to achieve eventual collection. The falsely collected or "overflexed" horse is so constricted that he loses normal function of the neck as a "balancer."

B. ANALYSIS BY FUNCTION OF THE PARTS OF THE BODY OF THE SEATED RIDER

1. Eyes

Where you look and how you look may largely determine how you sit. Both the direction of vision and means of altering it will influence the aspect of the whole upper torso. This is largely due to the relative weight of the human head.

The normal point of vision when riding should be straight ahead between the ears of the horse at a point somewhat above them. When sitting close to the vertical, the chin of the rider should be well tucked in so that the aspect of the head is perpendicular. *The temptation to look down at the horse should be avoided.* When we are driving an automobile, the normal point of vision is through the windshield in the lane in which we are driving. At times it is essential that we shift vision. We may have to look down at the dash to check an instrument. If so, we glance down briefly and immediately return our attention to the lane in which we are driving. We know that if we keep looking down at the dash we are placing ourselves in danger of a serious accident. *It is a fallacy to assume that because the horse is a living creature instead of a machine, the rider does not have to look where he is going.* At all times the rider must be directing the horse by conscious will, implemented by the aids. The willingness to permit the horse to assume the initiative of direction signifies the resignation of the rider and he becomes a mere passenger.

Human beings have several options in changing direction of vision. The first is the resource of the muscles of the eyes.

Fig. 25: Left, rider looks down with head only. *Right, rider looks down with* shoulders.

We are able to look up, down, left, or right without moving the head. We do this, laterally, continuously while reading, for example. (The horse has similar optical muscles but seldom chooses to use them. He prefers to turn his head.)

By rotating the head on the column of the neck, we are able to look up, down, right, or left, *without moving the shoulders.* The movement or rotation of the head alone does not affect the center of gravity of the rider and therefore does not influence the performance of the horse.

On the contrary, looking down *with the shoulders* will cause a rounding of the back down to and including the lumbar region. The loin will lose its effectiveness as an impulsor force because in this position it cannot be "braced." The center of gravity of the rider will involuntarily be sent forward and so influence the performance of the horse. Both esthetic and practical posture of the rider will be lost (fig. 25).

Another factor to be considered is that human peripheral vision covers a satisfying area. *It is not necessary to look at something in order to see it.* If we look at a potential danger point, such as a hole that we do not wish our horse to step into, it is not necessary to keep looking at it. If it resides in the peripheral vision, we will easily avoid it.

2. Mouth

While you are riding, the mouth should be predominantly softly closed. Most breathing should be done through the nasal passages. There are several good reasons for this. First let us consider the "esthetic." The rider with open mouth and slack jaw presents a poor spectacle indeed. On approaching an obstacle, the rider with open mouth is prone to open it even more, lending a general impression of surprise and alarm to his whole aspect. Here we discover what is often a truth. *What is esthetically satisfying is also what is eminently practical.* The liability of attempting to breathe through the open mouth while riding is that the inside tissues of the buccal cavity soon dry out, producing considerable discomfort. We discover also that breathing through the mouth while riding is also more exhausting than breathing *shallowly* through the nasal passages.

I well recall that while competing in my first horse shows I had not learned this little secret. I became known as a game and happy competitor who came into all his fences smiling gaily. The truth was somewhat different. What I was wearing was a fixed and gruesome grin. When the tissues of the inner borders of the lips become sufficiently dehydrated, it becomes impossible to close them over the teeth!

We said above that the mouth should be *softly* closed. The softness or tenseness of the lips quickly reveals to the experienced instructor whether the rider is truly relaxed or not. If the lips form a hard, compressed line, one can surely assume that the sternomastoid muscles of the neck are tense and rigid. This sympathetic rigidity proceeds down the muscles of the back *to the seat.* The horse is instantly conscious of it. He is unable to yield elastic performance because the rider is unable to accompany him.

Fig. 26: Bring arms up together over head.

3. Neck

The neck is a vertical column arising from the cradle of the shoulders, which can be carried tall or short, regardless of the innate physical structure of the rider. There is another favorite saying among horsemen: "Sit as though someone were suspending you by the ears." The simple meaning of this is *sit tall*. Do not permit the column of the neck to sink into the shoulders. The most useful exercise for obtaining this is to raise the arms, bringing them together over the head. When you bring them down, *continue to sit tall* (fig. 26).

As implied in the discussion of eyes, the muscles of the neck should be soft and relaxed so that the head may rotate freely in any direction.

Fig. 27: Left, shoulders open. Right, shoulders closed.

4. Shoulders

A very short experiment with your own body will serve to demonstrate the difference between "shoulders open" and "shoulders closed." *All riding should be done with shoulders open* (fig. 27).

Because of various influences of crowded city life, many urban dwellers develop poor posture. The shoulder-closed, rounded-back "slump" walk is a common sight in large cities. The walk of most professional athletes is, on the contrary, one of open-shouldered erect dignity. Primarily it is because they know how to *breathe*. When the shoulders close and the upper back rounds, the lungs are forced inward. Proper respiration becomes both more difficult and more exhausting. When shoulders are open in erect posture the lungs are normally expanded and have an opportunity to do their proper respiratory work. There will be no need to "suck for air" in order to get sufficient oxygen. Shallow breathing through the nasal passages will permit satisfactory respiration without undue exhaustion. The extremes of these two methods of breathing will become even more apparent at altitudes over five thousand feet, especially for habitual dwellers at sea level. At sixty-five hundred feet there is approximately thirty percent less oxygen present than at sea level. This factor formed one of the greatest doubts of the 1968 Olympics, held in Mexico City at an altitude of seventy-five hundred feet.

5. Arms and Hands

I am often asked about the proper length of reins. The answer to this will vary somewhat in the case of every paired horse and rider, since the conformation of horses differs and so do the proportions of individual riders. The soundest precept is that in all normal riding the elbow should be well in advance of the rider's hipbone unless the forearm is actively in use. This represents an open triangle, the base of which is the distance between the elbow and the iliac crest of the rider's hip. When it is necessary to activate the forearm, this triangle moves toward closure. If the elbow is normally carried *at* the hipbone, it will have to pass behind it in order for the forearm to function. *This should never happen!* Fig. 28 illustrates the difference in these extremes.

Seen from top view, the arm from shoulder to wrist should form a light, inward curvature (fig. 29). This will induce a direct line from the elbow to the horse's mouth. Any breaking *out* of the wrist joint will interrupt this connection. Therefore the articulation of the wrist should always be inward. The proper functioning of the entire arm as well as the articulation of the wrist is largely governed by two groups of muscles: the deltoid of the shoulder and the brachioradialis muscle of the forearm. It is absolutely essential that these two groups of muscles be relaxed if the articulation of the wrist is to be soft and sensitive and the rider is to develop "good hands."

In equestrian lore there is much mysterious mumbling about "good hands." It is implied that this is a God-given faculty that one is born with or without.

Fig. 28:
Elbow at proper
place.

Elbow retracted
to hip.

Elbow behind hip.

I do not agree.

From my years of observation I conclude that "good hands" are the result of identifiable physical factors and that any rider of normal sensitivity can develop them if he goes about it intelligently. First of all we repeat another but less well-known

Fig. 29: Proper inward curvature of arms and wrists
Wrist rotates inward and downward only

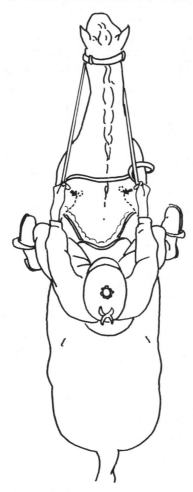

horseman's adage: "Good hands are the result of a good seat."
Although quite true, this adage is hardly explanatory. It implies that the rider in equilibrium (in the balance seat) *will
not look to the reins for support*. The reins are to *support and
influence the horse, not to support the balance of the rider*!
Therefore, the rider who has developed his independent equilibrium has the opportunity to develop "good hands." I would
define the latter as hands that are able to maintain a light and
sympathetic contact with the horse's mouth, to accompany the
variable movements of his head and neck, and *tactfully to influence* him when necessary *without fighting him*.

The sensitivity here implied depends almost entirely on the
relaxed articulation of the wrist. This is immediately impeded
if the muscles of the shoulder and forearm are tensed.
Especially the tensing of the muscles of the forearm will
lend a stonelike quality to the wrist, and the sensitive horse
will immediately fight it.

It should be remembered that the snaffle, unlike the curb,
which acts by leverage on the bars of the jaw, acts on the
tissues of the commissure of the lip. These are probably the
most sensitive tissues the horse has to give you. *Do not abuse
them*!

It is true that there are horses with "hard mouths." Most
of them have been made so by the hands of inconsiderate
riders or trainers. Constant and heavy pull on the snaffle will
bring nature to the defense of the horse. Scar tissue will be
built up on the tissues of the commissure in order to deaden his
sensitivity and relieve his pain. He will fail to respond satisfactorily. The horse is best influenced by a series of signals
that relax *within a constant contact*, keeping the tissues of his
response area alive.

The proper means of holding the reins, both snaffle and
double bridle, one hand or both, is shown in figs. 39 and 40. In
all cases the thumb presses down on the second segment of the
index finger and acts as a stop on the rein. The extra rein (bight)
is always carried to the right side of the horse's neck. The hand
should be carried at the vertical, with thumb up, never at the

horizontal, although it is quite permissible that the vertical hand be tilted inward up to 30 degrees. There are two main reasons for carrying the hand vertical. The first is that, thus held, the elbows remain closer to the rider's side. They have far less tendency to splay outward and to flap, especially when approaching a fence. The second reason is that the vertical position of the hand permits a much greater range of motion in the wrist than does the horizontal hand. The height of hands should be only a few inches above the withers.

In terms of communicating with the horse's mouth the rider has the following resources:

The first is the simple pressure of the thumb downward on the segment of the index finger. This may serve to actuate the rein as much as half an inch if contact is constant.

The second is the pressure of the thumb and the closure of the fingers at the same time. The normal riding position is with fingers loosely closed. Opening the finger joints serves to destroy intimacy of contact with the horse's mouth. The closure of thumb and finger joints at the same time in a repeated close-relax pattern will serve to actuate the rein almost double the extent of thumb alone.

The third resource is the articulation of the wrist inward and downward. Obviously this exerts an even more forceful signal. Even when not activated, it is the wrist joint, more than any other, which, if loose and relaxed, serves to maintain constant and sensitive contact with the horse's mouth.

The last resource is the activation of the forearm by closing the space between elbow and hipbone.

In appraising the above resources it should always be remembered that the *lightest* aid is desirable if it will produce the response. If the horse will not respond to the above resources of the hand, *he will not respond to anything stronger.* Up to now we have been speaking of the resources of the hand to influence by means of equestrian tact. Strength of pull is not involved. To employ the power of the rider's shoulder as a pulling force is a useless gesture. This involves a tug of war

between the strength of rider and horse. In a test of strength
the horse will obviously win. It is worth remembering that
among the great international riders of the world are slight
girls who weigh as little as one hundred and fifteen pounds.
Clearly they do not achieve their admirable results by strength.

6. The Upper and Lower Back

The normal riding position of the back is concave. There
are circumstances under which a convex back is employed.
This will be explained specifically under the sitting trot. The
rider with open shoulders will be able to maintain a concave
back much more easily than the rider with closed shoulders.
Given a hollow back, the angle of the loin, at the articulation
of the waist, will project out in opposition toward the cantle
of the saddle. It is this position that enables the rider to "brace
the back," which actually means to turn the lumbar region
into an impulsor force.

The horse responds to two physical impulsor forces on the
part of the rider. One is the closure of the legs on the flanks.
The other is the driving force of the lower back of the rider
when it is "braced." Just as the impulsor legs are applied in
the halt, so, too, the lower back is also braced at the halt in
order to drive the horse up into the bit.

At the posting trot the lower back activates the pelvis and
lifts the rider's seat just the amount necessary to clear the
action of the horse. During the act of posting one never raises
the shoulders. All impulse comes from the lumbar region implying a loosely articulated waist. The pelvic structure is sent
upward and forward on a diagonal line, putting the crotch
slightly above the level of the pommel. It will be seen, then,
that the action of posting will be satisfactory only if the upper
back is maintained *concave* (fig. 30). Each rise of the post
should be accompanied by a push into the heels, momentarily
increasing the flexion of the ankle. In this way the stirrup,
which is under the instep, acts as a trampoline and assists the
rising action of the rider.

Fig. 30: Rider at rise of posting trot with concave back.

It is in the sitting trot that the convexity of the back is employed. Bouncing at the sitting trot is a discomfort for the rider and a greater one for the horse. At the point of impact the kidneys of the horse are relatively close to the surface. The horse will finally object to having his kidneys pounded by the seat of the rider.

In order to avert this, it is first worthwhile establishing what actually happens in a mechanical sense. It would appear that the rider is banging on the horse. Actually the reverse is true, although the effect is the same. In the first action of the trot the horse drops out from under the rider. The rider fails to follow him down. The horse then rises and hits the rider's seat. The problem is to follow the horse down and to

Fig. 31: Sitting trot. Left, rider follows horse down *with convex back. Right, rider follows horse* up *with concave back.*

follow him up without leaving the seat. This may be accomplished by making the waist a loose articulation and using the back alternately convex and concave (fig. 31).

The principle will become apparent if you do the following: Place a rider with a reasonably flexible waist on a horse, sitting in the balance seat with concave back. Request that by articulation of the waist he makes his back alternately as convex and concave as possible, without moving the seat. Place the end of your index finger at the point of greatest convexity, level with the waist. You will discover that at the point of greatest concavity the rider's waist is some five inches from your finger. This five inches represents displacement in a horizontal plane. At the sitting trot it may be converted to *vertical* displacement in a one-to-one ratio. When the horse is dropping out from under, the convex back of the rider follows him down. When he is rising, the concave back follows him up.

There will be no bouncing.

7. The Seat and the Sitting Bones

The contact of the sitting bones will depend on the orientation of the pelvis. If the line of the lumbar region be exaggerated toward the cantle, the rider will be resting major weight on the crotch. On the contrary, if it *lacks* angle toward the cantle, the rider will be sitting on the fleshy parts of the buttocks. In between these two extremes is the proper base of support—the sitting bones. The sitting bones serve to influence the horse and may be used bilaterally or unilaterally. Bilateral use implies equal weight on both sitting bones in order to drive the horse straight forward on the track. In unilateral use, the major weight is put onto one sitting bone to influence the horse to the same side. As long as applied, it will result in a turn in the same direction. It is employed as an aid, therefore, for turns until the turn has been completed. In curvatures it it constantly applied as long as the horse is to be kept in curvature.

In the gallop depart it is one of the essentials of diagonal aids. In putting the horse to the canter on left lead one employs the right leg and left hand. However, at the moment before departure, the weight of the rider is shifted to the left stirrup and the left sitting bone. It follows that unilateral use of the sitting bones plays a large role in the change of leads.

During riding the sitting bones are at all times in contact with the saddle, the only exceptions being the periods of elevation of the posting trot and always when employing the forward seat.

Although the lateral muscles of the stomach play a minor role in riding, they are employed at the posting trot and are therefore worthy of mention. It is beneficial to wear an actual belt while riding rather than any form of beltless breeches. Since during the act of posting the stomach muscles are required to stretch, they should be completely relaxed in order to function properly. If there is no support by belt, the stomach muscles are quite apt to tense up in order to defend themselves.

8. The Thigh

The inner thigh is the area of contact of most intimacy with the horse. It is here primarily that the horse telegraphs to the sensitive rider what he is doing and often what he is *about* to do. Riding in the balance seat there is *no need for pressure* of the inner thigh. Indeed, pressure of the inner thigh tends to squeeze the rider upward and destroys the "deep seat." The effect is somewhat like squeezing a tube of toothpaste.

The rider who is behind his center of gravity in the old-fashioned seat or in the contemporary American saddle seat will find that his only area of contact on the inner thigh will be the high point of the sartorius muscle, which is a minimal area. In the balance seat the thigh is put forward and down. This rolls the sartorius muscle *back* and creates a broad area of contact.

It is true that some hot-blooded Thoroughbreds may be rated down by successive pressure of the inner thigh. It will have no effect on a colder-blooded horse.

9. The Knee

The knee, like the inner thigh, is an essential area of contact. *Under no circumstances should it separate from the flap of the saddle in any phase of equitation.* This does not mean that the knee is nailed in one spot. In actual fact it rotates in a small circle. As in the case of the inner thigh, *there is no need for undue pressure.* Too much pressure with the knee will evert the lower leg and lose the contact between the inner calf and the barrel of the horse. Especially in the case of approach to fences, any space between the knee and the flap represents a signal danger to the rider's security.

The only circumstance in which I can imagine need of pressure of the knee is if one elects to post without stirrups. Otherwise the balance seat makes such pressure both superfluous and unfortunate.

10. The Lower Leg

The inner calf is an area of variable contact with the barrel, all the way down to the anklebone. The extent of this contact will vary with the temperament of the horse being ridden and the type of work being done. An extremely sensitive horse will often ask for little contact with the lower leg, a less sensitive horse for more. It may be noted that green riders when starting out find more sense of security with more contact of the lower leg. As balance improves, the need for this security becomes negligible.

In doing dressage involving lateral work especially, the passive leg will often have to be *off* the horse. It will be brought closer to increase forward motion. (See Chapter XV on advanced dressage.)

Fig. 32: Left, lower leg, normal position. Right, lower leg impulses behind girth.

When the lower leg is carried too far out from the barrel, there is almost no way of applying the leg sensitively. The use of the lower leg as an impulsor should be a squeeze-and-relax sequence, *not a kick*. The horse receiving a kick will react brusquely and his progress will be interrupted. When the lower leg is carried in intimacy there is only a small space to close in order to apply it. When a large space has to be quickly bridged the result is usually a kick (fig. 32).

Fig. 33: Ankle broken out.

11. Function of the Ankle

The ankle, as noted earlier in this book, plays an over-whelming role in the security of the rider. As adjuncts to the seat, the main security of the rider will reside in the proper flexion of the ankle and the contact of the knee. This is especially true over fences. The foot should be so placed that the base of the stirrup is just ahead of the broadest point of the sole of the boot as it narrows toward the toe. Contact of sole is always on the inner branch of the stirrup, with all excess stirrup width to the outside. The heel must be well down below the level of the toe, taking the major weight. In other words, the ankle must be well flexed. During riding the ankle must not be *rigidly* flexed to its limit. It should be elastically flexed and able to move rhythmically with the action of the horse.

The ankle joint should be *broken* out as well as flexed. Seen from front view the foot will cant toward the outside. This can be achieved only if the predominant weight is on the inside branch of the stirrup. The canting out of the foot at the ankle will put the inner calf in much more intimate contact with the barrel of the horse than is possible with the straight foot (fig. 33).

VI

Natural and Artificial Aids

A. GENERAL COMMENTS

The aids form the language of communication between the rider and the horse. When that language becomes corrupted, the horse will be in doubt as to what is wanted of him. It is therefore essential that if communication is to be kept open and clear, the aids must be applied both correctly and consistently. Reverting to the guiding rule of reward and punishment, it is well to remember that by far the greatest reward one can give to the horse is the relaxation of the aid. The physical aid at the moment of application is a discomfort to the horse. It should be relaxed the instant the obedience has been yielded even if it is to be reapplied shortly thereafter. The constant reapplication of a given aid, when required, must be in the cadence of stride of the gait in use.

It is found convenient to divide the aids into natural and artificial. Under the natural aids we include the voice, body weight, back (loin), seat, legs, and hands.

Artificial aids include reins, spur, crop, martingale, or any other mechanical gadget.

B. USE OF NATURAL AIDS

1. Voice

The voice is a perfectly acceptable aid and there is no reason not to employ it provided it is used with discretion.

It should be remembered that a dressage test is an exception. During the test the voice is not permitted, at least to the extent that the judge can hear it. If you have taught your horse to go forward on the clucking of your tongue, this may be permitted if inaudible to the judge. Predominantly, the horse is expected to respond to the physical aids.

Discretion in use of the voice refers to riding or hunting in company. It is considered a great discourtesy if you use your voice in such a way that it affects the behavior of horses other than your own. It is hunting custom, while the Master is casting hounds, for all huntsmen to sit their horses as quietly as possible. A loud command to your horse at this time might well set a number of horses in motion. Conversely, when hounds are in cry you may encounter difficulty in slowing your horse. If you shout "Whoa!" and six other horses stop, you will quickly lose whatever popularity you previously enjoyed in the hunt.

Horses rapidly become accustomed to verbal commands and are prone to respond even if the verbal command comes from other than their rider.

When I instruct a number of riders in the ring, all the horses are listening alertly for my voice commands. At my command "Stop!" all horses stop instantly, usually before the riders have time to put in their aids. If one happens to be teaching the aids to the halt, this becomes a disadvantage. Under these circumstances I explain that I will use the word "Red!" to indicate the halt, since the horses do not understand it.

The voice, as previously pointed out, may easily serve as reward or punishment. It is not necessary for the horse to understand the words you use. He will know by the tone of your voice whether you are praising him or bawling him out and react accordingly.

Another function of the voice is to calm the frightened horse if he is alarmed by some phenomenon he may not understand. A pat on the neck and a few reassuring words will often do more than anything else to settle down a nervous horse.

The voice may serve to *reinforce the physical aids.* A horse is most often schooled initially on vocal commands before being introduced to the physical aids. Therefore, in using the voice as reinforcement you are harking back to his early schooling impressions. In any use of voice command the key is *consistency*. Always use the same inflection and tonality, for it is these latter that the horse recognizes rather than the word itself. The same word pronounced differently may mean nothing to him.

2. Body Weight

The function of weight displacement of the rider has been previously alluded to in a discussion of the balance seat. We here consider it as an aid, since the horse *tends to follow the weight displacement of the rider*. The rider may displace his body weight forward, slightly backward, or to either side laterally.

Forward displacement of weight (light seat or forward seat) will influence the horse to increase speed and lengthen stride. Slight backward displacement serves to oppose forward motion of the horse (diminish speed, halt, or reinback).

Forward displacement is employed going *up* steep slides. Figs. 34a and 34b show proper position of the rider going up and proper position going down.

Note that in going up the rider is flexed forward, with heels down, but that he is stretching arms out to the point of the horse's shoulder, giving complete freedom to the horse's head and neck. This is necessary at all gaits but particularly at the canter, where the motion of head and neck is greatest when ascending.

Fig. 34a: Correct position, ascending slide

In going down, rider is still flexed forward but all weight is in the heels. Now there must be a firm contact with the mouth of the horse to give him support as he descends and to regulate his speed. It is quite all right for him to ascend at his speed *but he must descend at yours.* At any point of his descent you should be able to halt him if necessary. Obviously, the descent should be made as straight as possible. Coming down a steep slide with the horse at an angle is dangerous.

I find that green riders readily accept the need of going forward in the ascent but are invariably amazed to be told to do the same in a steep descent. They assume that one should lean far back going down, which is, as a matter of fact, the worst thing one can do.

A brief analysis will show that the forward-inclined rider at the descent has his center of gravity over the horse's mass, which is a base of support. Functionally, the horse's forelegs act as the brake for his descent and have no need to move from side to side. The haunch, on the contrary, must be free to move laterally when the hocks are folded under it, in order to preserve equilibrium. Taking predominant weight off the haunch allows the horse the necessary lateral freedom of the quarters. The center of gravity or predominant weight of the rider is closer to the forehand, which is braking and supporting the mass in its descent.

Lateral displacement (from the base of the stirrup up) will influence the horse to one side or the other for a turn, until the turn is executed. Continued lateral displacement will be used for circular figures. (See Chapter VIII on basic dressage—

Fig. 34b: Correct position, descending slide

aids to the volte.) It is noted that lateral displacement does not imply a collapsed hip.

Once the rider has come to appreciate the function of lateral displacement, he will seldom be tempted to employ the reins for what can be accomplished both more easily and more gracefully by weight displacement.

A demonstration of this fact can easily be made on a well-schooled horse: Tie off the reins and begin a serpentine on straight lines, using half the width of the arena. Touch the rein only when absolutely necessary. On coming to each U turn *lean to the inside.* On the straight path sit straight. A little practice at this exercise will show that the well-schooled horse needs almost no rein effects to navigate these U turns successfully.

Since the green rider almost invariably believes that his only means of directing the horse is by means of the reins, the importance of weight displacement cannot be overemphasized.

A safe rule in horsemanship is: *Never use the reins for an effect that another aid can achieve!*

When the horse is on curvature, the displacement of the rider should be no more and never less than the cant of the horse off the vertical (fig. 35). In sharp radius curves, such as those encountered in pole bending or barrel racing, the angle of the horse to the ground may be extremely acute. *The rider still must be at the same angle as the horse* if he is to accompany him. The same thing of course holds true for the motorbike rider.

3. Back (Loin)

The "bracing" of the lower back acts, like the legs, as an impulsor force to send the horse forward. It can, of course, be braced only when the area above it is concave. It is a particularly strong impulsor force in achieving the extended trot posting.

It is used invariably as an aid to the halt, forcing the seat as deep down in the saddle as possible, using the closed legs as leverage.

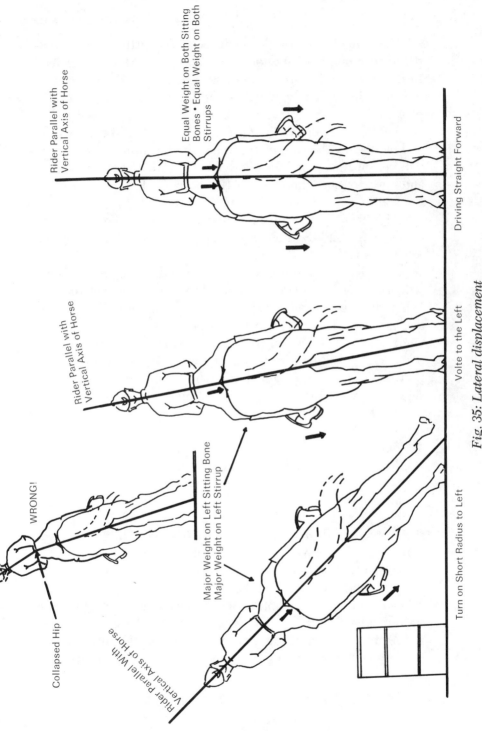

WRONG!

Collapsed Hip

Rider Parallel With
Vertical Axis of Horse

Major Weight on Left Sitting Bone
Major Weight on Left Stirrup

Rider Parallel with
Vertical Axis of Horse

Rider Parallel with
Vertical Axis of Horse

Equal Weight on Both Sitting
Bones • Equal Weight on Both
Stirrups

Turn on Short Radius to Left

Volte to the Left

Driving Straight Forward

Fig. 35: Lateral displacement

The function of the lower back at the sitting trot has already been pointed out under "The Seat of the Mounted Rider." In this case, by means of alternate concavity and convexity of the area immediately above it, it is absorbing vertical displacement.

It also functions to take up the displacement of both walk and canter. In the case of the walk, the flexibility of the waist will permit the angle of the lower back to rhythmically change and thereby accommodate to the horizontal displacement of the walk.

The displacement of the canter is an arc. If the seat is not to leave the saddle, the lower back must thrust and receive exactly as it does in a swing.

Whether or not it is at right angles to the spine of the horse will of course depend on the angle of the whole pelvic structure. When driving straight forward (bilateral use) it will be at right angles. It will be slightly unilateral if the whole pelvis is angled laterally. Even in the act of posting, the lower back is not completely at right angles to the horse's spine. If one is posting on the right diagonal, the whole pelvis will be directed slightly toward the side of the diagonal, since the thrust of the horse will be from the left hind.

4.   Seat

It has previously been remarked that in contrast to other parts of the body, the seat is relatively fixed; the actual point of contact is the two sitting bones when the rider is properly seated. There are only two circumstances under which the sitting bones will not be in contact with the saddle: one is 50 percent of the time during the act of posting and the other is the rise of the forward seat. At all other times the sitting bones are in contact, influencing the horse either bilaterally or unilaterally. Pressure on both will be absolutely even to drive straight ahead and unilaterally accented for lateral influence.

A proper understanding of the function of the sitting bones is easily achieved if you put your hands, palms up, under your seat and sit on them. Sit evenly and then press alternately with either sitting bone. What you feel is exactly what the horse feels *through the saddle!*

The greatest stabilization to the quarters of the horse will be exerted when the force of the seat is straight down. Therefore dressage riders sit *vertically.*

A good example of unilateral use of the sitting bones is the gallop depart on diagonal aids. (For an explanation of diagonal versus lateral aids, see below.) In putting the horse to the canter, left lead, we shift the weight to the left stirrup and the left sitting bone.

Those of you who have seen the riders of the Spanish School of Vienna demonstrate the change of leg at every stride may have marveled that no physical aids are discernible. The rider seems to sit like a statue. It would almost seem that the horse is changing leg to the music, but of course he is not. The aids have merely become highly subtle and refined. The rider is mainly achieving the changes by alternate pressures of the *sitting bones.*

5. Legs

(a) Bilaterally as Impulsors

Both legs applied well behind the girth act as impulsors to send the horse forward. Application of the impulsor legs *does not imply a kick!* They are squeezed and relaxed in cadence with the stride. When the leg is applied at the area of the girth, it encounters the solid ribs of the horse and his response will be minimal (in terms of forward motion). Well back of the girth it finds the floating ribs where the horse is much more sensitive.

In applying the leg it is not necessary either to evert the knee or to raise the heel!

When the knee loses contact with the flap of the saddle, the security of the rider is instantly diminished. When the heel rises, the effect of the leg is largely destroyed. (See Chapter XV on Dressage—High School, particularly section on aids to the leg yield and two track.)

A little practice will show that it is quite possible to apply the leg without everting the knee since only the lower leg from the knee down is in motion. It will also be seen that the foot may preserve the *same ankle flexion*. In this way it is the *back* of the heel that touches the horse, not the side. Reinforcement by spur will depend only on how much the toe is turned out and how high the spur is worn on the heel.

(b) Unilaterally for Displacement

Use of the individual leg may displace the whole horse laterally or only one portion, depending on where it is applied. If the left leg is applied close to the girth, it displaces the entire horse laterally to the right. If the same leg is applied well behind the girth, it will displace only the quarters to the right. This is how a turn on the forehand to the left is obtained. With each application of the left leg behind the girth the horse should

Fig. 36: Bending the horse into corner of the arena

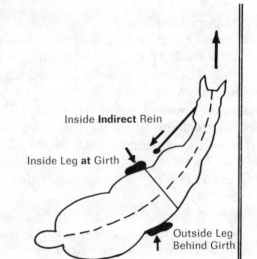

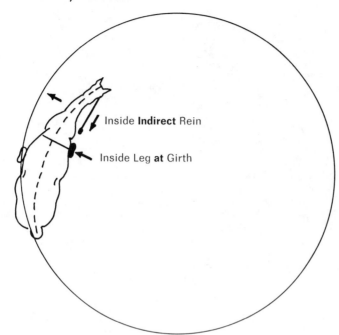

Fig. 37: Corrective aids
Forehand bearing in on volte to the right

take one step with quarters to the right, pivoting on his right forefoot, which is picked up and put down in place.

Another example of necessary use of one leg is the horse who is tracking left in the arena and attempts to cut the corner because he does not want to bend his body. Pressing with the left leg, *at the girth,* plus use of the left indirect rein, will bend him into the corner (fig. 36).

Another example: Horse on volte to the right diminishes the circle by bringing in the forehand. Rider uses inside right leg to put the forehand back on the circle (fig. 37).

Still another use of corrective single leg: Horse on volte to the right straightens his spine by displacing quarters to the left. Rider's left leg acts behind the girth to reestablish the curvature (fig. 38).

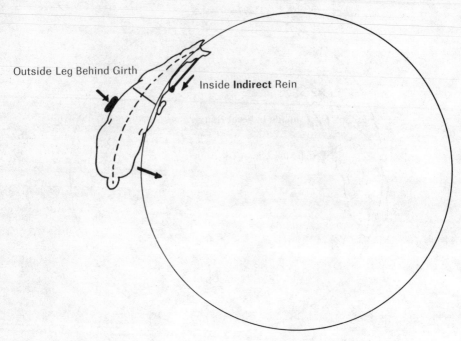

Fig. 38: Corrective aids, eversion of haunch—volte to right

The single leg may also act as an assistor to regulate the
effect of the active leg. Example: Turn on the forehand to the
left (haunches moving right). On application of the active left
leg the horse overresponds and attempts to take more than
one step with the quarters. The passive right leg, normally at
the girth, immediately moves behind the girth to slow the
motion of the quarters.

6. Rein Effects (Hands)

Since the hand holds the rein, we here make the transition
from the natural to the artificial aids.

Figs. 39 and 40 show the proper way to hold snaffle single
reins, double reins in both hands as well as in one. In all cases
the bight (extra rein) is carried to the right side of the horse.

Fig. 39: Above, proper way to hold snaffle reins in one hand. Right, proper way to hold snaffle reins in two hands.

Fig. 40: Above left, proper way to hold double reins in two hands. Left, proper way to hold double reins in one hand.

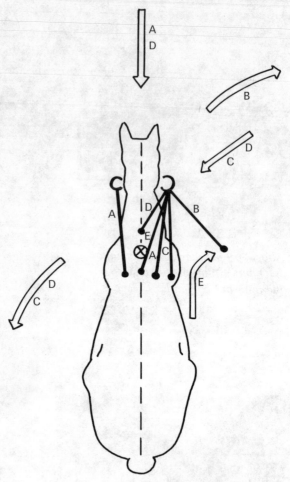

Fig. 41: The five rein effects

There are only five basic rein effects. They are all illustrated in fig. 41.

Rein effects are divided into *direct effects* and *indirect effects*. In direct rein effects the horse responds in the direction of pull of the rider's hand. In indirect rein effects the response of the horse is *not* in the direction of pull of the rider's hand.

(a) Direct Rein of Opposition

Used with both hands, straight toward either side of rider's midline. Purpose is to decrease speed, stop, or reinback. It is in *opposition to forward motion.*

(b) Opening or Leading Rein

Used singly to effect a turn to either side. A direct rein effect in which the response of the horse follows the hand. The extent to which the rein is open or leading may vary considerably and still remain a direct rein effect.

(c) Indirect Rein

Used singly. As shown in fig. 41, response of the horse is now no longer in the direction of the hand.

Example of use: We return to a previous example of horse, tracking left in the arena, who attempts to cut the corner. The combination of the pressure of the left leg *at* the girth plus the *left indirect rein* will easily bend the horse into the corner. Were one to use the left opening rein it would pull the horse *out* of the corner. If one were to use the right leading rein, it would pull the horse's head to the right and destroy his left curvature.

(d) Indirect Rein of Opposition in Front of Withers

Used singly. As shown in fig. 41, result of this rein is both to swing forehand of horse to the opposite side and to oppose forward progress at the same time.

Example of use: Riding in pairs tracking left, the inside rider on approaching corner now has not only to bend his horse into the corner but at the same time to slow forward speed, enabling the rider on his right to keep abreast. Combination of the left leg at the girth with the left indirect rein of opposition in front of the withers will accomplish this.

(e) Indirect Rein of Opposition Behind Withers

Used singly. As shown in fig. 41, response of the horse is

to invert the shoulder on the same side.

Example of use: Primarily used to achieve the "shoulder-in." (See Chapter XV, Dressage—High School.)

While there are only five rein effects, like five musical notes they can be combined in many ways to achieve various effects. In the employment of the aids the following general rules will be found useful:

1. Always the *lightest* aid to get the desired effect. Never use two pounds of pressure when one pound is sufficient.
2. The active aid initiates the movement.
3. The assisting aids are used to assist the primary aid to get the movement.
4. Correcting or opposing aids are used to correct or modify the original movement.

(f) An Explanation of the Terms Active and Passive

The above terms are relative, not absolute. A passive leg is not necessarily *absolutely* passive. It is merely awaiting response to the active leg, ready to act when necessary. A passive hand is almost never completely passive. The joint of the snaffle forms the connection between the pull of the two hands. In the case of the curb or pelham the solid bar will so function. What the active hand takes in rein the passive hand yields *with support and resistance*. If the passive hand became *truly* passive, the force of the active hand would be doubled.

C. USE OF THE ARTIFICIAL AIDS

1. Spur

The spur is used to reinforce the leg. If properly used, it is a valid and indispensable aid to complete horsemanship. In many quarters there is a prejudice against the spur, possibly as a means of cruel and unusual punishment of the horse. It is true that improper use or abuse of the spur can cause the horse discomfort. However, the crop too can be a means of abuse. This is no reason not to carry one.

I am forced by observation and experience to the conclusion that many instructors, in the United States and Canada particularly, do not wish to bother to teach the use of the spur and therefore discourage their students from using it until some distant future, which seldom arrives. This reminds me of what a young lady from the United States told me. She had taken a year of equitation at a Middle West college as one of her regular studies. She had never cantered. "Cantering," she told me, "doesn't come until the second year!"

Among the Olympic jumping teams of the world there are hardly any riders who do not wear spurs. After years of observation in several countries, I can at the moment recall exactly one—from Argentina. Go to an international dressage show. You will find all the dressage riders in spurs. This is the class of riders that has developed the subtlest and most refined aids. Only a small percentage of dressage horses will respond satisfactorily in work at two tracks without use of the spur.

Severity of the spur is controlled by three factors:

a. Length and shape of spur
b. Height worn on the heel
c. Position of the toe

The spur should be of normal length. A short, so-called "dummy," spur has little effect on the horse. When worn high on the heel, resting on a spur support of the boot, it is most effective. When slanted down to the bottom of the heel, it is "softest." When the toe is held in normal riding position (less than a ten-degree eversion), only the side of the spur will touch the horse, and it will never be used unintentionally. The further the toe is everted, the more marked the effect of the spur will be. The rider who learns to control toe position is always in command of the use of the spur.

2. Crop

As the spur reinforces the leg, the crop reinforces the spur. It is used for three purposes: as an urge to forward movement, as a punishment, and as a schooling device (training whip).

In terms of the first two purposes it should be used decisively and always *back* toward the quarters on one or both sides. The rider should strive to be equally adept with the crop in either hand. Under no circumstances should the crop be used vigorously on the shoulders or forehand. This discourages forward motion, and with crop forward the rider may inadvertently injure the eye of the horse. Using it forward may well result in the horse's becoming crop-shy. The horse should respect the crop but have no inordinate fear of it. The crop should be used only with deliberation and good timing and only when necessary. It should never be used merely to relieve anger and frustration on the part of the rider. Overuse will both diminish its effect and make the horse neurotic.

The sluggish, uncollected horse will often come alertly to attention if the rider is merely given a crop to hold, without using it. In terms of the force of application of the crop it must be remembered that the pain threshhold of the skin of the horse is entirely different from that of human beings. When you pull hairs to dress the mane of the horse, he obviously feels no pain.

The use of long crop or training whip for schooling purposes has nothing in common with either forward urge or punishment. Tapping with the training whip at the point of application of the leg will often get the message through to the green horse that the rider wishes him to yield to the tap and finally to the leg. It is often used from the ground when the horse is "in hand" to increase collection. It is also used from the ground on shoulder and alternating forelegs when teaching the reinback.

Included under artificial aids are any gadgets man employs to reinforce the natural aids. During many dark periods of history man has been the inventor of scores of artificial devices capable of inflicting great cruelty on the horse. Invariably the purpose was to make up for a lack of horsemanship. Obviously, the list of all artificial devices is far too long to examine in detail here. However, because of their widespread use, the running and standing martingales should not be omitted.

Fig. 42: Running martingale gives leverage to rider's hands.

The running martingale is an extremely useful and humane device for the hunter or jumper going in snaffle bridle (fig. 42). It gives leverage to the rider's hands by breaking the line between hand and mouth and exerting a slight *downward* pull on the commissure of the mouth. It is an aid in collection on the snaffle if not overused. If adjusted to proper length, with rings sliding on reins, *it does not inhibit the horse's jumping ability.* The horse with proper running martingale has complete freedom to extend his head and neck during the bascule of the jump.

The standing martingale, on the other hand, is quite a different kettle of fish. It has a fixed length from girth to chin.

If adjusted short enough to function at all, *it will inhibit the horse's bascule during jumping.*

I was both surprised and shocked, when assisting judging at a Middle-Western horse show, to find that some 70 percent of the horses in the open jumping classes were wearing standing martingales. The few riders I questioned were unable to give me any sane reason for their use.

Again, it pays to look at the world's most talented riders. Observation at any large international jumping event will disclose that nine out of ten Olympic jumping team riders use running martingales. The appearance of a standing martingale is unknown.

In polo the standing martingale performs a useful function. Naturally, the polo player does not jump. He is often forced to make abrupt stops and turns while carrying the mallet in one hand and four reins in the other. At these sudden stops, which are often near-collisions, the standing martingale prevents the horse from suddenly raising the head dangerously high.

3. The Diagonal Aids to the Canter

No discussion of aids in this context would be complete without a clear explanation of the difference between lateral aids and the diagonal aids employed here at the Escuela and by most advanced riders of the world.

Were I to make an estimate of all the riders who have come to the Escuela over the years, I would say that 80 percent of North American riders with previous formal instruction have been taught lateral aids only.

The difference:

Lateral aids imply that the leg and hand used to achieve and maintain the canter act on the same side of the horse.

Diagonal aids imply that the leg and hand act on opposite sides.

E.g.: To take up the gallop depart on the left lead with lateral aids (fig. 43a), the rider uses the right leg behind the

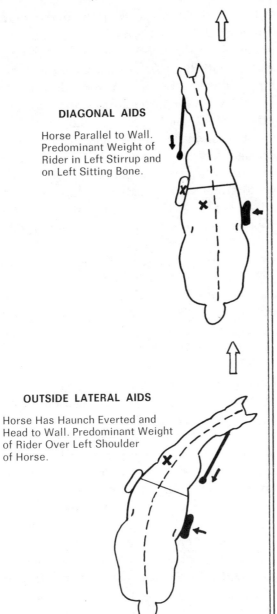

DIAGONAL AIDS

Horse Parallel to Wall.
Predominant Weight of
Rider in Left Stirrup and
on Left Sitting Bone.

Wall of Arena

OUTSIDE LATERAL AIDS

Horse Has Haunch Everted and
Head to Wall. Predominant Weight
of Rider Over Left Shoulder
of Horse.

*Fig. 43: Aids to the gallop
depart.*

girth and pulls the horse's head to the *right* with the right hand. At the same time he displaces his body weight forward and over the left shoulder of the horse, essentially throwing him off balance. Leading with the left fore will give the horse a base of support for the displaced weight of the rider. Notice in fig. 43a that his haunch must be displaced in from the track. Should he be permitted to continue to canter in the position of departure, with major tension in the rider's right hand, he will canter crabwise and also have difficulty seeing where he is going. Therefore, the rider who has taken the gallop depart on lateral aids now has to straighten his horse so that forehand and quarters are both on the track. Cantering in circular figures or turns, his head is being influenced in a counter-curvature to his spine.

E.g.: To take up the gallop depart on the left lead with diagonal aids (fig. 43b), the rider uses the right leg behind the girth, calls the horse with his *left* hand and at the moment departure is desired, shifts weight to the left stirrup and left sitting bone. Notice that the horse is square on the track parallel with the wall of the arena. *He proceeds at the canter without change of position.* Since the active hand is the *inside* hand, there should be no counterposition of head on turns or in curvature. In a proper canter on a turn, there will be a constant curvature from poll to dock.

There is of course a valid function for lateral aids to the canter. Properly it should be a transitional phase for the young horse who has had his initial schooling from the mounted rider. Once he is satisfactorily taking up his lead by being essentially thrown off balance, he should then logically be introduced to diagonal aids so that he can initiate his canter *in balance*.

Why is this final step so often ignored in North America? The answer has to lie in either plain laziness or economics. In highly industrialized countries the most costly commodity is skilled human labor. Economically a horse represents his original cost plus maintenance plus the man-hours of schooling invested.

We often find that it is necessary to school a horse for a full year or more before we can allow a student rider to mount him. Admittedly it is not economical, but since, in the last analysis, it is the horse that does the teaching, I have never found any shortcut to the problem. It is a fact of life.

It should be remembered, however, that a horse who receives most of his original schooling on the longe (see Chapter XI on Longeing) *never has to be taught lateral aids.* Since all his early work has been on curvature (in the direction of forward motion), it will be found that when finally mounted *he will respond naturally to diagonal aids.*

Advice? Longe your horse!

Most horses, by the way, have an inborn preference for the left lead. During the period of gestation the foal is curved *to the left.* Newborn colts, when they find their feet and are able to canter, prefer to strike out on the left lead (note the relationship of lead to curvature). Most racetracks of the world are run counterclockwise. Most Thoroughbred track horses therefore understand only the left lead, as you will quickly discover if you buy a horse off the track.

D. INDEPENDENCE OF THE AIDS

There seem to be three stages in the progress of the rider as far as use of the aids is concerned. The first is independence, the second coordination, and the third is the balance of the aids. In Chapter II, Preliminary Exercises on the Ground, we have called attention to the fact that the unconditioned reflex is the enemy of independence on the part of the rider. Until this sympathetic reflexive reaction on the part of the body is conquered, there is no independence. If the right leg is to act, *there must be no involuntary motion of the left leg,* nor of any other part of the body.

In searching for an apt analogy I have hit upon music and the problems encountered by the child learning to play the piano or organ. There is a minimum of two staffs to read. The

fingers of the left hand must play one set of notes while the
fingers of the right hand play a different set. In the case of the
organ, the feet must simultaneously play a third staff.

The first difficulty that the child encounters is that the
fingers of each hand want to do the same thing. By dint of
much practice he discovers that he can make the two hands independent and think for both of them at the same time. The
beginning rider learns independence in much the same way.
Essentially, the process consists of the suppression of unconditioned reflexes.

E. COORDINATION OF THE AIDS

After the child at the piano has achieved independence,
the teacher must convince him that music depends on a mathe-
matical beat that constitutes its time. Now the two hands must
coordinate in order that both conform to the time and rhythm.

The rider developing coordination of the aids now discovers that a given leg effect must coordinate, for example,
with a given rein effect in order to achieve a specific result.
They must coordinate in *time* and within the cadence or
rhythm of the gait being ridden.

F. BALANCE OF THE AIDS

When the rider has truly achieved the balance of the aids,
horsemanship begins the transition from a sport to an art. This
balance is based essentially on a developing sense of relative
stresses and forces. It will partake of the esthetic to the extent
that the effect achieved will be an *individual* expression of the
particular rider and will constitute his "style."

VII

Mounted Exercises
at Walk and Trot

A. PURPOSE

The objectives of gymnastics on the horse are to supple and relax the body of the rider, to diminish automatic reflex actions, and to *increase his sense of balance and security.*

B. AT THE WALK

1. Slow circles with the right or left arm. The arm is extended up, moving in a downward direction in a continuous circle with elbow and wrist relaxed. The eyes follow the hand so that the head is made to rotate on the neck (fig. 44).

Fig. 44: Walk—Exercise 1

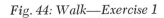

Fig. 45:
Walk—Exercise 2

Fig. 46: Walk—Exercise 3

2. In rhythmic count, turning the head, look right, look left, look up, look down (fig. 45).

3. Circles with the points of the toes: feet out of the stirrups, circle out with the toes by rotating the ankle joint. Circle, similarly inward with the toes (fig. 46).

4. In rhythmic count with feet out of stirrups, flex ankle joints to raise point of toe as high as possible. Extend foot to point toe down as far as possible (fig. 47).

5. Leg flexion. With feet out of stirrups fix knees in saddle flap. Raise legs alternately back to the horizontal and return (fig. 48).

6. Elevation of the legs. With feet out of stirrups and balanced on buttocks, raise both legs in semi-flexion until both feet are at height of hips. Maintain this position briefly and then lower legs to repeat exercise (fig. 49).

Fig. 47: Walk—Exercise 4

Fig. 48: Walk—Exercise 5

Fig. 49: Walk—Exercise 6

Fig. 50: Walk—Exercise 7

7. Trunk flexion. In rhythmic count flex trunk forward and down with arms semi-flexed toward points of horse's shoulder. Seat and legs are maintained in correct riding position, thus pressure on heel is increased. Head should be raised and eyes should be front. Back of rider should not hump in this exercise (fig. 50).

8. Trunk rotation. Sitting vertical with arms extended, rotate rhythmically to right and left as far as possible (fig. 51).

Fig. 51: Walk—Exercise 8

Fig. 52: Walk—Exercise 9

9. Remount. Bring right leg over to the left side. With right hand holding top of right stirrup leather and reins in left hand, pass right leg under left and *in one continuous motion*, remount (fig. 52).

C. AT THE TROT

1. Rise and stand in stirrups. With *lower leg well back and ankle flexed*, find your balance. Back should be arched and

Fig. 53: Trot—Exercise 1

shoulders open. When you resume seat do so by extending the posterior and come back to the seat slowly and voluntarily (fig. 53).

2. With reins knotted, sit the trot. Extend arms laterally and in rhythmic count bring them together in front of you and then behind you (fig. 54).

Fig. 54: Trot—Exercise 2

Fig. 55: Trot—Exercise 3

3. With reins in right hand, flex forward at the waist and touch the horse with left hand as near to poll as possible. Come back to vertical, extend arm behind, and touch haunch as far back as possible. With reins in left hand, repeat with right arm (fig. 55).

4. Taking the reins in left hand, bring right hand to toe of left boot *without moving leg position. Look ahead.* Change reins to right hand and reverse (fig. 56).

Fig. 56: Trot—Exercise 4

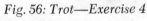

Fig. 57: Trot—Exercise 5

5. With feet out of stirrups, squeeze with the knees and post. This is a most useful exercise but a demanding one and should be done only in short intervals (fig. 57).

6. Extend arms forward, looking straight ahead. Try to reach for snaffle rings with each hand (fig. 58).

Fig. 58: Trot—Exercise 6

Fig. 59: Trot—Exercise 7

7. Without changing leg position lie back relaxed and rest head on rump of horse (fig. 59).

VIII

Basic Dressage
Exercises Performed in Group

A. DESCRIPTION AND CUSTOMS OF THE DRESSAGE RING

Official specifications for the standard dressage ring are set by the International Equestrian Federation (F.E.I.). The placement of the letters as well are specified and should be uniform throughout the world (fig. 60).

For reasons of space limitations or economy, a smaller-dimension ring is often built, but it should be remembered that it is not possible to execute the same maneuvers in a smaller ring as in a standard one.

The standard ring is a rectangle, 20 meters wide by 60 meters long. It may be portable by means of low connecting, movable fences and portable letters. This is the type most often used for high-level dressage tests. It may be permanent, in which case the side walls will be higher and slanted inward and preferably wooden-boarded to prevent contact of the rider's boot with the wall. It may be a covered riding hall or *manège*, in which case it is desirable to have at least two overhead angled horizontal mirrors on the long sides and similar vertical mirrors on the short sides so that the riders may observe and criticize themselves both in profile and front view.

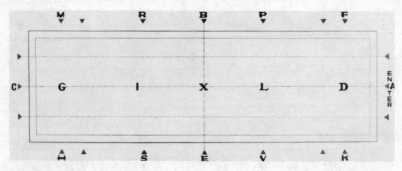

Fig. 60: F.E.I. standard arena (Escuela Ecuestre Dressage Teaching Device).

For the health of the horses concerned, it is essential that the footing be soft and resilient, and if exterior, that good drainage be provided. Usual footing is a covering of sand over a clay base. Sea sand is preferable, if available. If creek sand, it should be mixed with generous quantities of salt to prevent packing. Other desirable additives are fine wood shavings, ground cork, or rice husks. This footing should be raked smooth at the end of each day's work. Letters should be large, clear, and visible.

The track on which most work is done is an area one meter wide, following the four walls. The inside track, often used for passing either in the same direction or opposite, is an adjacent area one meter in width (fig. 60). The entrance is at A, and the judges' stand, elevated and outside the ring area, is usually at C. The line AC, which bisects the width, is called the medium line. Doors invariably open *out* for reasons of safety.

The line BE, which bisects the length, is called the center line. The broken lines shown on the diagram are called the quarter lines, since they divide the width into four segments of five meters each. All of these lines are of course not visible but theoretical, as are the interior letters, D, L, X, I, and G. The long sides of the ring are referred to as the major sides and the short sides as the minor sides. The major sides are useful for extension and the minor sides for collection. It is easier to collect a green horse when he can see only twenty meters of track ahead and easier to extend him when he can see sixty.

Traffic is controlled in the ring mainly by the rules that apply to passing. In the Western Hemisphere, passing in opposite directions is done by maintaining the right, passing left shoulder to left shoulder. (In England and Ireland, for example, the *left* hand is maintained.) Originally, of course, the left hand was preserved since swordsmen and lancers met from opposite directions, right hand to right hand.

Even in the Western Hemisphere there is one exception to maintaining the right hand when passing in opposite directions. This is the rule that the superior gait has the right to the track.

For example, you are proceeding on the right hand at the walk and another rider is approaching you at the walk on the left hand. (You are proceeding on the right hand when the inside of the ring is to your right and vice versa.) Normally you will move to the right to the inside track and pass left shoulder to left shoulder. However, should the other rider be coming at the walk and you at the trot, he is expected to move to the *left* and give you the track. The same applies if he is at the trot and you are at the canter.

The rules of traffic lead naturally to the courtesy or etiquette of the dressage ring. The rules are extremely simple and based primarily on considerations of safety. Where one or more horses are working in a ring one does not enter on horse without permission. One stands one's horse at the door and yells, "Door!" When the instructor or trainer considers it safe, he will ask you to enter. Similarly one does not take one's horse out of the ring without doing the instructor the courtesy of announcing a wish to retire.

The use of the voice as an aid in the ring is entirely permissible. (It is prohibited in a dressage test.) *However*, the voice must be so regulated that it will not affect the performance of other horses working nearby. This particular courtesy of the ring extends naturally to group work in the exterior and even more importantly to the courtesies of the hunting field.

The functions of the dressage ring may be briefly expressed as follows: It is primarily a *school* for horses and riders and in England it is called "the school," but its use is not limited to the schooling of green horses and riders. It is used throughout the life of horse and rider to attain more and more finesse in the realms of advanced horsemanship and also to reschool horses spoiled by inept handling.

Basic dressage as employed in group practice consists of two types of maneuvers. One is *simultaneous* and the other is *successive*. As the words imply, in simultaneous exercises all riders execute the same maneuver at the same time in unison. In successive exercises the maneuver is performed in single file, headed by the rider designated as number one or head of line. In relation to successive exercises, however, it is well to note that it accomplishes nothing merely to allow your horse to follow and imitate the horse in front of him. He must work individually under *your* command and in response to *your* aids.

B. SIMULTANEOUS EXERCISES

1. Cross the Ring (Fig. 61.)

The diagram shows five riders coming on the left hand,

Fig. 61: Cross the ring (simultaneous)

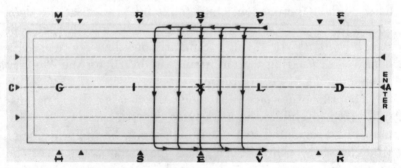

turning 90 degrees on command, crossing simultaneously, and again turning 90 degrees to take up the same hand on the opposite side.

Orders for all exercises in the ring should be given by separation of syllables. The first syllable gives riders a chance to prepare their horses, and at the final syllable the aids are applied and the maneuver executed in unison.

Crossing the ring involves a 90-degree turn at either side. There is of course a right and wrong way to turn a horse 90 degrees. It may be done by merely using an opening or leading rein, without combining other aids. But when so turned, two unfortunate results will be noted. The first is to surprise the horse's mouth, since he has had no forewarning of intention. The next is that when so turned, he turns with a straight spine, as a ship would, and will very likely bring his haunches into contact with the wall of the ring.

Proper Aids to Turn 90 Degrees

On final syllable of command put major weight in the left stirrup with left leg at the girth, and major weight on the left sitting bone. The right leg touches the horse lightly *behind* the girth and the left hand exerts leading left rein.

With these aids the well-schooled horse will bend his dorsal spine around your left pivot leg and turn fluidly and comfortably. When 90 degrees to the wall, the horse should be driven straight across the ring by sitting evenly on both sitting bones, equal weight in both stirrups, and equal contact in both hands. Velocity and cadence should be exactly the same as it was on the track.

2.   Cross the Ring and Change the Hand (Fig. 62.)

This is the same maneuver as the former with the exception that on reaching the opposite major side we turn opposite, constituting a change of hand.

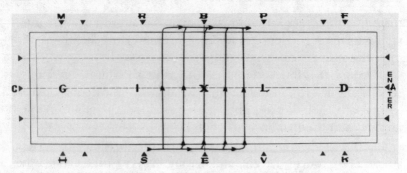

Fig. 62: Cross the ring and change the hand (simultaneous)

3.   The Volte (Fig. 63.)

The volte as shown in this diagram is a circle of ten meters diameter being performed simultaneously by three riders. The objects of the volte are as follows: The horse must be willing to curve his spine around the inside leg of the rider and perform a *true circle*, his spine forming an arc of the circle traveled.

(a) Aids

When departing from the track for curvature to the left, the rider puts major weight in the left stirrup, left leg at the girth, and major weight on the left sitting bone. The right leg should be behind the girth to impulse and ready to control displacement of the quarters. With the young horse it will be best to carry the left or inside hand lower than the right (by the distance of a fist). The left hand will be the active hand and the rein effect will be the *indirect* rein. (See Chapter VI on the Aids.) The right hand will be the passive hand, but note that these are relative rather than absolute terms. A passive hand yields what the active hand takes *with contact and support*. Were the passive hand to yield completely, the effect of the active hand would be doubled. Traveling a circle of reduced diameter the horse will no longer be 90 degrees to the ground but will cant to the inside, as will a bicycle on curvature. The rider must displace body weight—from the stirrup up to the

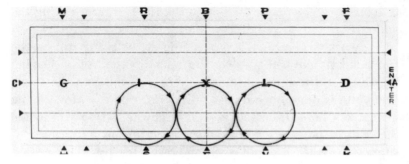

Fig. 63: Volte at 10 meters (simultaneous)

inside—in order to be at exactly the same angle to the ground as is the horse (fig. 35).

Lateral displacement is achieved by pressure on the inside stirrup, *not* by collapsing the hip (fig. 35).

(b) Correction of Errors in the Volte

If the horse attempts to bring his forehand in (in this case to the left), he should be pushed out by the inside leg at the girth and a left indirect rein. He should not be *pulled* out by a right rein as this will destroy his curvature (fig. 37).

If the horse attempts to straighten his spine by displacing his quarters to the outside, he will no longer be able to travel the circle properly. The correction is the outside leg *behind* the girth (fig. 38).

(c) General Comments

The volte may be initiated at ten meters diameter for less experienced riders. Like most of the other maneuvers discussed in this section, it may be done at walk, trot, or canter. At whatever gait, it must be executed at the *same cadence and velocity* as previously employed on the track. This involves the previous *rating* of the horse on the track. Distances between riders as requested by the instructor must be maintained consistently, indicating that all riders are proceeding at the same velocity. Should one rider close the space in front of him by failure to rate his horse, he may collide with the rider in front during the volte.

If work on the track is proceeding at the rising trot on the track and a volte is requested, the rider *sits* the trot on leaving the track and resumes posting only on returning to the track. The volte is done once unless otherwise ordered. Most of the maneuvers here discussed are done at the *sitting* trot when that gait is indicated. Only the seated rider has a firm base of support and therefore full command of his leg aids. The posting rider is unseated 50 percent of the time and therefore has only partial command of the leg and seat aids.

It is worth observing that the horse entering into curvature has a natural tendency to decrease velocity and therefore change cadence. This must not be permitted. Depending of course on the temperament of the individual horse, it may well be necessary, at the moment of entering curvature, to increase leg pressure, in effect telling the horse not to decrease velocity.

The horse that properly performs the volte will leave *two tracks*, the hinds following the curvature in the track of the fores. The horse that displaces and straightens his spine will likely leave *three tracks*.

4. The Semi-volte (Fig. 64.)

This is a half volte done at six meters. On completing the

Fig. 64: Semi-volte (6 meters, simultaneous)

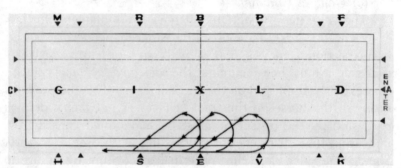

half volte the rider returns to the track on the oblique line (45 degrees), constituting a change of hand.

Aids

The aids for the semi-volte are identical with those of the volte, as far as the curvature extends. When driving the horse straight forward on the oblique, the rider must sit straight with equal weight in both stirrups, equal weight on both sitting bones, and equal tension in both hands.

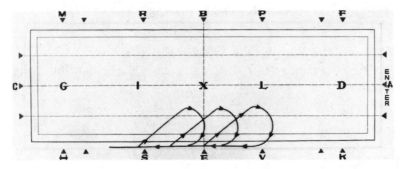

Fig. 65: Inverted semi-volte (6 meters, simultaneous)

5. The Inverted Semi-volte (Fig. 65.)

This figure is identical with the semi-volte but executed in the inverted form. The rider *leaves* on the oblique and *returns* on the half circle.

Aids
Identical with semi-volte.

C. SUCCESSIVE EXERCISES

1. Cross the Ring by the Length (Fig. 66.)

To be executed on the medium line, one rider following another.

Aids
Identical with "Cross the Ring."

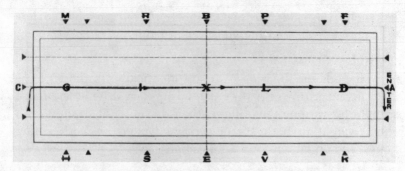

Fig. 66: Cross the ring by the length (successive)

2.   Cross the Ring by the Width (Fig. 67.)

To be executed on the center line, one rider following another.

Aids
Identical.

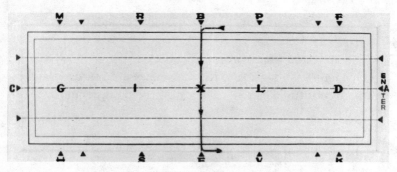

Fig. 67: Cross the ring by the width (successive)

3.   Cross the Ring by the Length and Change the Hand (Fig. 68.)

To be executed on the medium line.

Aids
Identical.

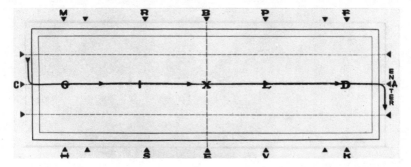

Fig. 68: *Cross the ring by the length and change the hand (successive)*

4. Cross the Ring by the Width and Change the Hand (Fig. 69.)
To be executed on the center line.

Aids
Identical

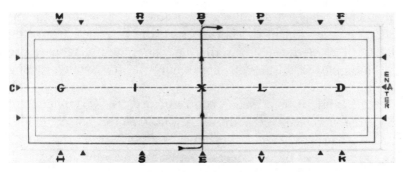

Fig. 69: *Cross the ring by the width and change the hand (successive)*

5. The Diagonal (Fig. 70.)
General Comments
The diagonal posts are located six meters from each corner.
They are designated by the letters M, F, K, and H. There are

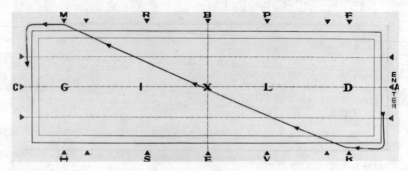

Fig. 70: Diagonal (successive)

two diagonal paths, crossing at center (X), and four diagonal directions. We may ride MK or KM or HF or FH.

To take up the diagonal in successive form, rider number one must first cross the minor side. Departure on the diagonal is made when the body of the rider is abreast of the designated letter.

Since the diagonal is often used to achieve the extended trot posting, it may here be appropriate to suggest some means of achieving same. Naturally a long line is preferable to encourage extension in the horse. Since the extended trot often takes time to develop, alternating continuing diagonals are often employed, meanwhile shortening the trot while crossing the minor sides.

Although it may seem contradictory, the extended trot requires *more* contact with and support of the horse's mouth rather than less. When the horse is confident of the rider's support, he will become more willing to reach out and extend. To encourage this with less-experienced riders we advise that the rider's hands be separated out to the line of the knees and indeed dropped down to the level of the knees. At the same time the horse must be urged forward by the rider's legs and lower back. The full extension of the trot is a beautiful and exciting air, since the forelegs of the horse are finally extended straight and the sense of impulsion is overwhelming.

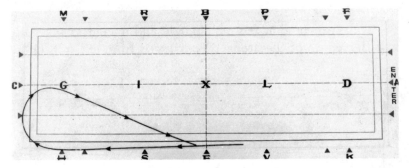

Fig. 71: Successive semi-volte

6. Successive Semi-volte (Fig. 71.)
(a) *Aids*
Identical with simultaneous semi-volte.

(b) *General Comments*
The successive semi-volte is always executed at ten meters, rather than six, and the maneuver takes up half the length of the arena. *Return* is at either B or E.

7. Inverted Successive Semi-volte (Fig. 72.)
(a) *Aids*
Identical.

Fig. 72: Inverted successive semi-volte

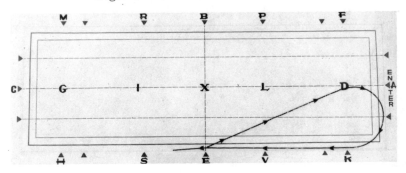

(b) General Comments

To be executed at ten meters only and maneuver takes up half the length of the arena. *Departure* is from either B or E.

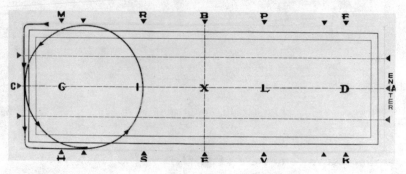

Fig. 73: The circle (successive)

8. The Circle (Fig. 73.)

Since the arena is 20 by 60 meters and the circle is 20 meters in diameter, three circles are possible in the ring. They are executed at either extreme unless the instructor specifies the circle at the center (fig. 74). The circle, unlike the volte, is continued until another order is given. In taking up the circle at the extremes, it is necessary first to cross the minor side. As previously explained, the diagonal posts are six meters from each corner. In a proper ring there should also be a marker

Fig. 74: The circle at the center (successive)

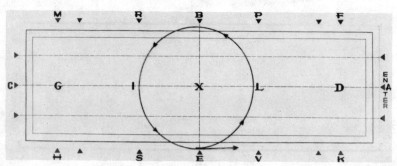

without letter four meters farther in on the major sides. This is the circle mark and is therefore ten meters from each corner. The circle is initiated at a given circle mark and terminated only at a given circle mark.

Aids

Identical with the aids of the volte. The only difference is that the diameter is greater.

9.   Change the Circle (Fig. 75.)

General Comments

On receiving the order, rider number one continues the circle to the next circle mark and from there takes a diagonal path through the center of the ring to the opposite circle mark. From there he initiates the circle at the other end on the opposite hand.

If the exercise is being performed at either the walk or sitting trot, no change will be involved. If performed at the rising trot, then the diagonal should be changed at X. When working in the ring at the rising trot, it is expected that we will be posting on the *outside* diagonal. When working on the left hand we will therefore be posting on the right diagonal. Specifically, we will be seated as the right forehand prints and elevated as the right forehand elevates. To try actually to look at the forehand of the horse in order to confirm rhythm will

Fig. 75: Change the circle (successive)

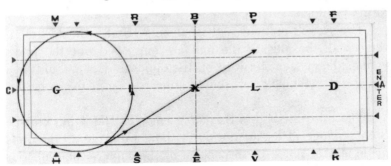

serve to destroy the seat and position of the rider. If one must orient visually, it is better to look at the shoulder blade of the horse, which moves largely horizontally. It will be back or retracted when the corresponding foreleg is printing and forward when the foreleg is lifting.

Far better is it for the rider to learn to *feel* which diagonal he is on. This may be attained by closing the eyes and questioning a competent observer on the ground. When one is posting on the right diagonal, the thrust of the horse is from the opposite hind. In order to change diagonals it is necessary either to sit a beat of the rhythm or elevate one beat. In this way one is automatically thrust onto the opposite diagonal.

If the change of the circle be done at the canter, then a change of lead will be indicated also at X. If cantering on the left *hand*, we will normally be cantering on the left *lead* unless we have specifically been requested to go at the counter-canter. (See Chapter XV on Advanced Dressage.) The reason for this is that only when going on the proper lead does the horse have a post of support from the inside hind on a turn. The horse not yet educated to the false or counter-canter is therefore in danger of falling on the turn when going on the false lead.

There are three accepted means of changing the lead in this case. The first may be called *transition by trot*. This means that perhaps three strides before X the horse will be induced to break from canter to trot. Immediately after X the opposite diagonal aids will be applied and the horse will take up the canter on the opposite lead. (See Chapter XIII on Gaits, Aids to the Canter.)

The second method is the *half halt*. Under these circumstances all the aids to the halt are employed but the horse is immediately sent forward on the opposite diagonal aids. To the observer the half halt should appear to be merely a hesitation.

The third method is the *flying change*. The flying change is the change of leg in the air without breaking stride. It is made at that phase of suspension of the canter when all four members of the horse are off the ground. It presupposes a high level of ability on the part of the rider and a horse of advanced dressage education. It is worth noting that many high-strung horses will perform flying changes of their own volition. Eliciting the flying change on request is quite another matter.

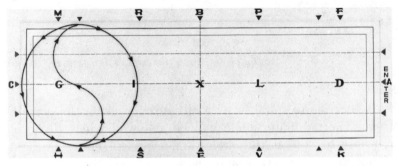

Fig. 76: Within the circle change the hand (successive)

10. Within the Circle, Change the Hand (Fig. 76.)
General Comments

In this exercise riders are seen in the circle coming on the left hand. On the order to change the hand within the circle, rider number one, on reaching the *next* circle mark, performs a figure S through the center of the circle and takes up the circle on the opposite hand.

The discussion of changes of lead at the canter given above in "Change the Circle" apply equally to this exercise. It is unlikely that this exercise will be done at the rising trot since it would accomplish little. It is worth noting that the curves of the figure S should be ample since the bend and counterbend of the horse's spine are essential to the proper execution of the maneuver.

11. Close the Circle, Open the Circle (Fig. 77.)
General Comments

On the order to close the circle, rider number one will begin

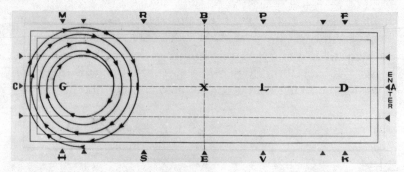

Fig. 77: Close the circle, open the circle (successive)

little by little to spiral in with all horses tracking the horse in front. The minimum circle will be achieved when all horses are nose to tail. As the circle diminishes, all horses must increase their curvature around the inside leg of the rider. As on all circular figures the spine of the horse must be a consistent arc from poll to dock. Under no circumstances should the head of the horse be permitted to locate to the outside, thereby breaking the arc.

When minimum diameter has been achieved, the instructor will give the order to open the circle. Rider number one will then begin little by little to spiral out until the full circle has been reachieved.

Fig. 78: Serpentine (successive)

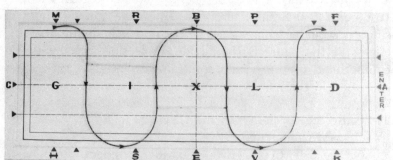

12. The Serpentine (Fig. 78.)

General Comments

The serpentine is properly done on curved lines. We have found it advantageous to begin the serpentine with inexperienced riders on straight lines as shown. In either form the serpentine in the standard ring consists of five loops, two and a half before the center line and two and a half after. It is continued in reverse until another order is given.

Many variants of the serpentine are practiced for schooling purposes. It may be done at the collected walk. It may be done at the rising trot, implying that the rider will change diagonals every time he crosses the medium line.

Variants may be based upon the medium line or the quarter line (naturally implying a greater number of loops). These variants are most useful for teaching the rider lateral weight displacement on short curvatures, or how to "go with the horse."

IX

Riding in Multiples

A. PURPOSE

It has been found that extremely valuable school work may be done in the ring by putting riders two or more abreast. The object of this is to encourage the rider to seek precision in all he does.

When working in single file, each rider is of course expected to exert as much command over his horse as though he were working alone. Too often the rider is tempted merely to follow the horse in front of him and imitate what he does in a desultory fashion. This becomes impossible when riding in formation. The mere problem of riders keeping their bodies aligned with each other demands that each must *rate* his horse individually and control its forward speed perfectly.

The rules that govern these changing formations are really quite simple, but they must be grasped by all participants if

Fig. 79: Increasing the front, single file to pair.

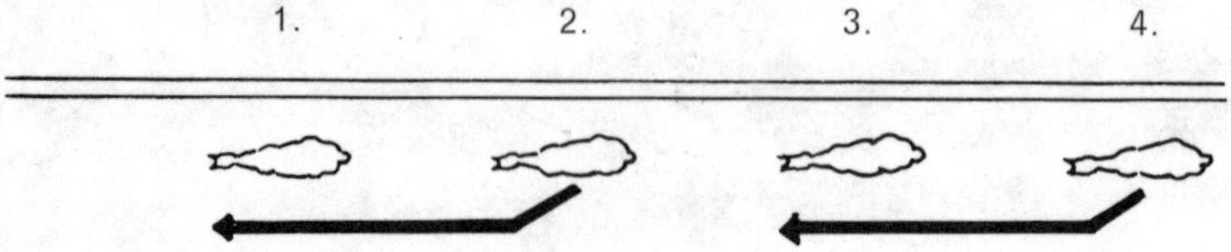

work is to be orderly and useful. The rules, of course, come out of cavalry practice governing formation riding.

B. INCREASING THE FRONT

When we go from single file to a greater number abreast, we say we are increasing the front. Fig. 79 shows eight riders going from single file to two abreast. Note that in increasing the front, riders invariably come *inside and forward* to pair up. In this case riders 2, 4, 6, and 8 must come in and up to pair with 1, 3, 5, and 7.

We may assume that all riders are one length apart and *going at the same forward speed.* That speed may be represented as "x."

In order to achieve pairing quickly and in an orderly manner, riders 1, 3, 5, and 7 must on order "By two!" immediately *cut their forward speed by half* ($\frac{1}{2}$x). Riders 2, 4, 6, and 8 must *double their forward speed* (2x) and come up on the inside.

Notice that in terms of spaces between pairs we now have triple the space we had in single file. On achieving pairs all riders immediately resume the original forward speed "x." *But the increased spaces must be maintained.*

Going from two to three, as shown in fig. 80, is only slightly more complicated. Inside rider of second pair must come up and in to form the inside third of leading triad. Third pair comes up and in to form second triad.

Fig. 81 illustrates increasing the front from two to four

Odd numbers ½ speed. Even numbers double speed.

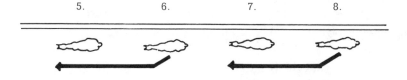

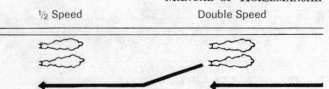

Fig. 80: *Increasing the front, pair to three* (above). *Decreasing the front, three to pair* (below, right).

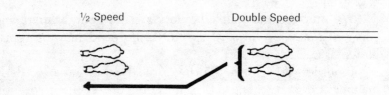

Fig. 81: *Increasing the front,*

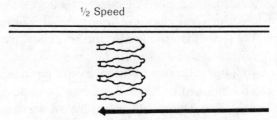

Fig. 82: *Increasing the front,*

abreast and fig. 82 illustrates four to eight abreast.

Riders in multiples are expected to keep as closely packed together as possible. They are to align by *riders' bodies* and ride leg to leg.

Fig. 83 shows the problem of eight riders turning the corner of the arena. As long as riders are 90 degrees to the wall of the

Double Speed

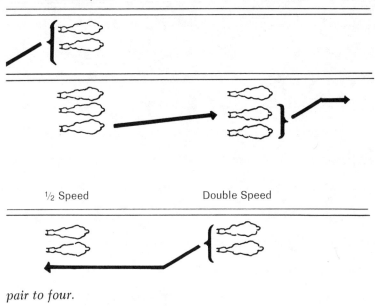

½ Speed   Double Speed

pair to four.

Double Speed

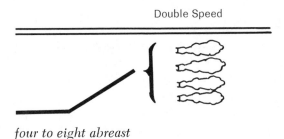

four to eight abreast

arena, all must go at the same forward speed. As the "spoke of the wheel" turns, the speed of riders will vary from one to eight. The inside or "pivot" rider has little more to do than turn in place while the outside rider must cover an extremely wide arc during the same time. When all riders are again 90 degrees to the wall, all must resume original forward speed.

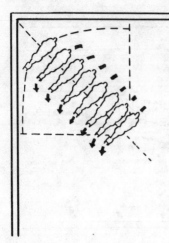

Fig. 83: Eight abreast, turn corner

Included in the useful work that may be done in formation of various multiples are voltes and semi-voltes. In all such maneuvers, of course, it is essential that the outside rider go faster than the inside rider. If a pair of riders are trotting on the track and execute a volte, the inside rider continues to trot and the outside rider canters to keep abreast.

Cavalletti work in units of two and four is most useful for both horse and rider. Low jumping from the trot through cavalletti is also most useful by two and by four.

A stadium obstacle of normal frontage will permit a maximum of five riders to jump abreast, provided they are properly packed together.

C. DECREASING THE FRONT

Exactly the opposite to the previous pattern must be followed. Fig. 8o shows decreasing the front from three to two.

D. CONTROLLING DISOBEDIENCES IN FORMATION RIDING

The first thing to stress is that riding packed together as closely as possible will minimize disobediences. The main ones to be dealt with are biting and kicking, and these may be intelligently controlled. Since horses are consistent in their vices as well as their virtues, the former become predictable.

If your horse shows a tendency to bite to his left he will not suddenly surprise you by biting the horse on his right. To prevent this vice, increase tension on the right hand and carry horse's head slightly to the right.

If your horse shows a tendency to "cow kick" with the left hind, tighten pressure on left rein and carry his head to the left. This will inhibit him from kicking out on the same side. Under no circumstances open up a space to your left. That space is an invitation for him to kick out on that side.

X

Faults the Horse May Acquire and How To Deal with Them

A. REFUSAL TO STAND STILL WHILE BEING MOUNTED

Naturally, the final solution to this problem is to reschool the horse to stand like a statue during the whole mounting procedure. This is usually easily accomplished in a routine of a few days.

However, since the unruly horse may indulge in vices during the mounting process, which may be of great nuisance to the rider, we should first consider the immediate defenses of the rider against these vices.

If the rider mounts facing backward, the horse may choose to curve the neck to the left and bite the rider's posterior. Very annoying.

Recourse: Shorten the off rein, since both reins are held in the left hand, preferably with a piece of mane. This turns horse's head to the right and prevents biting to the left.

If the rider mounts facing forward, the horse may choose to cow kick with near hind, at the same vulnerable posterior of rider, now facing opposite.

Recourse: Shorten the *near* rein, fixing head of horse to left, thus opposing hind with forehand. The horse with head bent to left is inhibited from kicking out with hind on same side.

Much better than these short-term defenses is taking the brief time necessary to teach the horse to stand properly during the mounting process.

First find a signal to advise the horse that you intend to mount. Vigorously slapping the stirrup leather against the saddle is as good as any, accompanied by the word "Stand!" Then get a supply of his favorite goodies, which may be apple, carrot, or whatever.

Divide the mounting process into its component parts, as described in Chapter III, under Mounting and Dismounting.

When he finally stands at attention during first phase of taking up the reins, praise and reward him. Go through each phase of mounting in the same way. Do not proceed to the next phase until he is standing perfectly at the previous phase. When you complete the final phase and settle down in the saddle, reach down and reward him, accompanied by generous verbal praise. *He is not to move forward even then until so commanded by the aids.*

I assure you that if this routine is faithfully followed, for the rest of his life your horse will stand at attention while you mount, waiting for the reward and praise he remembers.

The very tall horse can easily be taught, also, to assist the rider's mounting by fully extending the forelegs, making himself much lower. The rider taps with boot alternately on each pastern of forelegs until the horse yields. With adequate reward along the way the horse will extend the forehand. Once you are mounted, a preassociated signal will command the horse to elevate to normal height. In Mexico, where almost all riders are shorter than North Americans, almost every charro horse is taught to do this.

B. LACK OF RESPONSE TO LEG AIDS TO MOVE FORWARD

This is a most annoying vice, but as in the case of so many others, it should not be made the subject of a major clash of

wills if equestrian tact will prevail. If circumstances dictate
that a final clash of wills is inevitable, *the will of the rider must
prevail* or previous training will suffer a serious setback.
Usually, it will suffice to back the horse a few steps, turn him
suddenly, and give strong leg impulse to go forward.

C. REFUSAL TO LEAVE A GROUP OF OTHER HORSES

This phenomenon is known as the herd-bound instinct or
"magnetism." The horse is by evolution a herd animal who
invariably feels the most security in the company of his kind.
(See Chapter XIII, Gaits.)

Again, in this case, we resort to the expedient of breaking
up the disobedience by breaking up the attention span. Turn
him quickly in several circles and immediately drive forward
in the desired direction. *Do not ever permit even one challenge
of this particular disobedience.* Further, keep testing your horse
for independence. When riding in the country in company,
take him off alone, just to test his willingness to leave the group.

D. REARING

Much is made of this phenomenon and it serves to frighten
many riders quite unnecessarily. (This is often the horse's purpose.) The thing to remember is that what goes up must come
down. He is not going to stay up there! Just keep your cool.

Most important is to go forward at the waist as soon as the
horse rises. *Never lean back! Never pull back on the reins!* The
only inherent danger is that if the horse rears near enough to
the vertical and the rider sends his weight back, pulling back
on the reins, he may pull the horse over backward with some
danger involved, more for rider than horse.

With head to right (to protect bridge of rider's nose) reach
for horse's shoulders and receive him in the hollow of the left
arm and shoulder.

It is of course better to prevent this vice, if possible, before it occurs. To the knowing rider, the horse will often telegraph his intention to the rider's inner thigh by bunching the muscles of the forehand. Disengaging the right foot, stepping down on the right rein, and pulling the horse's nose into the ground will often discourage him.

For the confirmed rearer that nothing else discourages, I would advise the services of a professional trainer to pull him deliberately over backward. Note! Do not use your best saddle! Do not attempt it yourself unless you are absolutely confident of your ability to get clear in time! Very few horses, after the frightening experience of going over backward, are anxious to rear again. Naturally, all vices should be followed by immediate punishment even if it is nothing harsher than a slap on the shoulder and a bawling out. It should be remembered, however, that even a slightly delayed punishment is useless and therefore should not be indulged in, as it is no longer a means of correction but merely an indulgence of the rider's bad temper. If the punishment follows *immediately* on the disobedience, the horse will associate it. If it is even slightly delayed, he will not associate it and instead will consider himself the victim of mistreatment.

E. THE KICKER

This has been touched on previously. If the horse kicks to the left, carry his head to the same side.

F. THE BITER

Also previously alluded to. If he bites to the left, carry his head to the right and vice versa.

G. THE BACKER

Very often young horses taught the reinback too early in

their careers will use this as a resistance when they wish not
to learn or not to execute a more difficult maneuver. It can be
a vice most vexatious to the rider.

I believe that the best way of handling it is to *encourage*
him to back. Let him back the length of the arena—sixty
meters—*and help him.* As soon as you do, it will no longer
be a resistance and will cease to be fun for him. He will get
thoroughly tired of it. Put the legs in briskly behind the girth,
sit vertical, and he will be glad to go forward.

Or back him straight into a solid wall. *He will not go into
it!* His peripheral vision allows him to see it and he is not
about to injure his haunches deliberately.

It is probably worth recording that horses often indulge
in bluff to see how much the rider will believe of their intentions. If schooling is to progress, *these bluffs must be called!*

I recall an experience when schooling a green horse over
fences on the jumping field of a Mexican cavalry regiment.
The horse decided to run off with me and jumped over the
hedge that fenced the field and took off cross-country. I could
easily have stopped him by circling him, but I was frankly
curious. He headed straight for a two-story pile of dried corn-
stalks. He was telling me in effect that he had every intention
of plowing a tunnel through this mass and doing both of us
in. I just did not believe him, so I urged him straight into it
even faster. With no aid from me he swerved left within a few
feet of it. He was simply bluffing and I called him.

H. THE SLOW HORSE

For satisfactory group work in the arena it is essential that
all riders go at the same speed and that spaces between riders
be kept consistent. The horse with the slow walk, for instance,
if uncorrected, will find the space in front of him growing
constantly larger. He must be urged on with legs by the rider,
in the cadence of the stride. If at the walk, the legs should be
applied alternately as the stride of the foreleg on one side is

initiated. To impulse the trot both legs can be used simultaneously behind the girth. To impulse the canter the *off* leg is used singly behind the girth.

I. THE FAST HORSE

As explained above, the impulse must be applied *in cadence with the stride*. The same thing is true of the deterrent. A steady pull with both hands is not a true deterrent. The horse *will* respond to alternate calls from each hand activated by fingers or wrist and applied in cadence. This should be accompanied by vertical seat with pressure straight down.

J. THE RUNAWAY

The horse that "runs away" is of course indulging in uncontrolled motion. The reason is usually fright or frustration, although more often the former than the latter. Even several years of assiduous schooling will hardly erase the racial memory of sixty million years of evolution. During all these millions of years the horse survived by running away from danger. When pressed hard enough emotionally, he will still do so.

For this reason it is worthwhile employing equestrian tact and not pushing, especially the young horse, beyond the limits of either his physical ability or the duration of his attention span. Do not drive him to desperation. To the best of your ability try to protect him from fright. Perhaps you cannot prevent some maniac with a motorcycle charging past the arena with blasting exhaust, but you can put up a sign, warning such fools off.

In considering the problem of dealing with the runaway, the first thing to demolish is the myth of the TV horse opera. In the classic scene of the western opus, the heroine screams as her horse runs away with her. Our hero gallops abreast, reaches over with right hand, and plucks her on to his own trusty horse. Heigh-Ho Silver!

Well, it just doesn't happen!

The one thing not to do with a runaway is to try to chase him. If the frightened runaway hears hoofbeats coming up on him he will go twice as fast. In the case of a runaway, the first thing all riders should do is *stop*. There is no way of others giving physical assistance.

By far the easiest way to stop the runaway is by circling to either left or right. If the circles are made smaller and smaller, *the horse has to stop!*

Should the terrain make circling to left or right impossible, the next recourse is the "pulley rein." This consists of fixing the left hand and rein in the mane and coming up with sharp calls with the right hand.

The one recourse guaranteed not to stop a runaway is a steady pull on both reins.

More important than anything is for the rider to remain calm and attempt to calm the horse. A truly frightened rider will inevitably add to the fear of the already frightened horse.

XI

Use of the Longe

A. PURPOSES

1. To begin the education of the colt long before he is mature enough to mount.

2. To teach him to respond properly to all basic verbal commands.

3. To make him supple and flexible by working *in curvature*.

4. To provide him with a program of directed exercise that he would not take voluntarily, thereby building a magnificent and toned musculature that free exercise does not create.

5. To calm his inherent nervousness and initiate the equine-human partnership essential to riding.

6. To introduce him to cavalletti.

7. To initiate his free jumping capacity and to conquer his fear of various colors and shapes of obstacles.

8. To introduce him to the saddle and finally to the weight of the rider.

9. To finally and gradually introduce him to collection.

10. To reeducate the spoiled horse and to correct gait defects.

11. To exercise adequately any horse when for any reason it is impossible to ride.

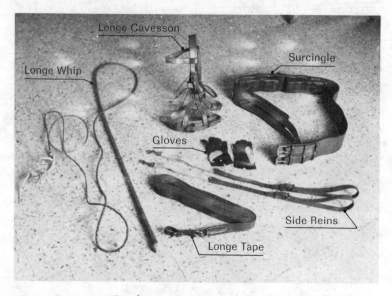

Fig. 84: Longeing equipment:
1. Longe whip, 2. Longe cavesson, 3. Surcingle, 4. Gloves, 5. Side
reins, 6. Longe tape

B. NECESSARY EQUIPMENT

1. A proper longeing cavesson
2. A longe tape with universal swivel
3. A longe whip
4. Surcingle and pad
5. Side reins
6. Gloves (fig. 84.)

C. EXPLANATION

Longeing improperly or with makeshift equipment not only may do the horse little good but may well harm his development considerably. Tying a clothesline to a snaffle ring does *not* take the place of a cavesson and longe tape!

The cavesson is so constructed that when properly adjusted it will not move while longeing. The noseband is constructed of curved, hinged, metal plates well padded inside so as not to injure the nose cartilage of the horse. The cheek-piece will not move over his eye. The noseband should have three hinged dee rings, one at center and one at either side.

The longe line should be a flat tape, about one and a quarter inches wide, of durable woven material. It should have a universal swivel at the end to keep from twisting while in use. It either buckles or snaps to the dee ring on the cavesson noseband.

Longe whips are flexible rod shafts about six feet long with an equal length of line and a lash at the end.

The surcingle, which goes over a blanket or pad, should have three dee rings, one top front and one at either side for eventual side reins.

The side reins should have an elastic section, allowing the head of the horse to stretch them when necessary.

Gloves should be used. Should the horse suddenly bolt the trainer may receive a bad palm burn.

D. TECHNIQUE OF LONGEING

When satisfied that cavesson and surcingle are properly adjusted, snap the longe tape to the dee ring of the cavesson. In the case of a green colt it is better to use the side dee ring. Later on only the center ring should be used.

When longeing to the left, the line is carried in the left hand and the whip in the right. The line should be folded in lengths of about two feet and grasped in the middle. It is thus simple to free one length of line and so increase the diameter of the circle. With an assist from the right hand, one may fold up line and diminish the diameter.

Since we are longeing to the left, the left foot of the trainer is the pivot. It is lifted and put down in place while the right foot walks around it. Concentrate vision on the horse

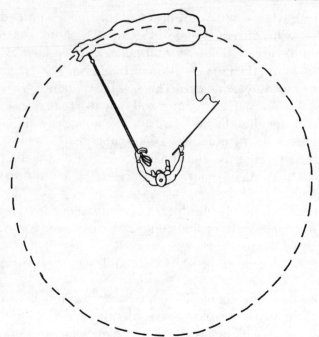

Fig. 85: Longeing circle

rather than the landscape behind in order to avoid dizziness. Fig. 85 shows the relationship of trainer to horse. Note that trainer is always *behind* horse's head at a point even with horse's shoulder. Therefore the little tugs on the line are a *deterrent*. The urge to go forward is the whip. Thus the horse is theoretically between the hands and legs of the eventual rider. The line represents the hands and the whip the legs.

Calls by the longe line, in addition to serving as a deterrent, may also be employed to maintain the curvature of the horse on the arc of the circle being traveled.

Note that these calls, when used at the trot, should be used at the moment when the *inside forehand is raised*.

At the canter they should be used when the *inside fore-hand initiates its transit*.

At the moment of printing, the call of the longe tends to

increase the weight on the supporting member and therefore leads to tendon strain. The more the horse is forced off balance, the more tendency there is to cross the outside member over the inside.

The whip should not be used threateningly so that the horse comes to fear it. *It is not a punishment.* It is merely an urge to go forward. The horse should merely respect the whip. When it is used actively it should be used low, with an upward motion, so that it encounters the horse just under the hocks. After a few such active applications, it is usually sufficient to point the whip, or at most alert the horse by the snap of the lash, in order to send him forward. Should the horse attempt to diminish the circle by coming in with the forehand, the whip can quickly point him off. Especially with the green colt, the trainer will have less trouble maintaining the circle if he faces a walled corner of the arena. If the trainer is fortunate enough to have an assistant, then the assistant will wield the whip at his off side and follow him. The trainer will then be able to hold reserve line in his off hand and contact the horse with the leading hand.

E. A PROGRAM OF LONGEING FOR THE YOUNG COLT OR FILLY

Longeing for moderate periods may be started any time between the first and second year, provided the colt is sound and strong.

It is to be expected that any colt of spirit will find cavesson and surcingle a new and upsetting experience in itself. When attached to the longe line he may well put on a grand performance of leaping and bucking. Let him do it. After he has used up some of this initial energy, settle down to work.

At this stage of the game, a nimble assistant is almost indispensable. At least, help will greatly facilitate and shorten the work.

In longeing to the left, put the assistant to the off side at the head of the horse to steady him. The assistant, with left hand, holds cheekpiece of cavesson.

We now introduce the colt to his first verbal command: "Walk!" Since the walk is the calmest of the three gaits, this should be the softest and least imperative of the three gait commands. At the word, the assistant walks forward and the colt walks with him.

We now must reemphasize the need for complete consistency in verbal commands. (See Chapter VI, Natural and Artificial Aids.) The commands must always be given with the same tone and identical inflexion in order to be understood by the horse.

After a brief walk on the circle, we are ready to introduce the next verbal command: "Stop!" The assistant halts and the colt stops with him.

The command for "Turn around!" is immediately introduced. The assistant, on command, leads the colt in a semi-turn, facing opposite. He then places himself outside with right hand on the left cheekpiece of the cavesson. We are now ready to proceed with the walk to the right.

Except under need of special circumstances, all longeing should be done for equal time in both directions in order to develop a balanced horse.

In longeing the green colt the period of work should be brief. His attention span, like that of a child, is limited. It is a new and demanding experience, physically. Fifteen minutes will be ample, daily, in the beginning. Over a period of several weeks, this period may be gradually doubled. It is far better to underdo than overdo. The bored colt will become stubborn and recalcitrant. One must have not only obedience but *cooperation*.

The next command the horse should be taught is "Come in!" For this it is essential that you throw the longe whip on the ground and that the horse come in willingly to you as you take up line. Pat him and reward him so that he will always be willing to come in to you.

Initial longeing of the colt should be done only on a limited diameter circle where the trainer has more control. Only as the horse becomes calmer and steadier should the diameter be gradually increased.

Only after the horse is walking, stopping, changing direction, and coming in calmly should he be introduced to the trot. When we introduce him to the command "Trot!" there should be a more imperative use of the voice, since the trot is a more vigorous gait than the walk. On command, the boy on the outside will immediately trot and the colt will trot with him. The patient procedure used at the walk is now employed at the trot, and work is alternated between the two gaits in both directions. What we are after at this point is a calm, *natural* trot, neither collected nor extended.

Only after considerable work at the trot, when the colt is taking his trot easily and calmly, should he be introduced to the canter. Naturally the voice command for "Canter!" should be the most imperative. The canter for the young colt should first be introduced *on the left lead*. During the entire period of gestation the foal is curved to the left. It is believed that this is responsible for the fact that it is more natural for most young colts to strike out on the left lead. (Most of the world's flat racing is done counterclockwise.)

Once the colt, with the encouragement of the assistant (who is still holding the cheekpiece), learns to initiate his left lead, he is of course then induced to take up his right lead. We are now working the horse at all three gaits in both directions.

Let us see how much he has learned. The boy now stands off-side at the head but does not hold the cheekpiece, but he still walks, trots, or runs on command as before. The colt should now merely imitate the boy. After this procedure has been repeated for a reasonable number of sessions, it is time to remove the assistant. The colt should now respond alone to all verbal commands, reinforced by light deterrent pulls on the cord and by showing the whip when necessary.

Fig. 86 shows progressive introduction of the cavalletti at

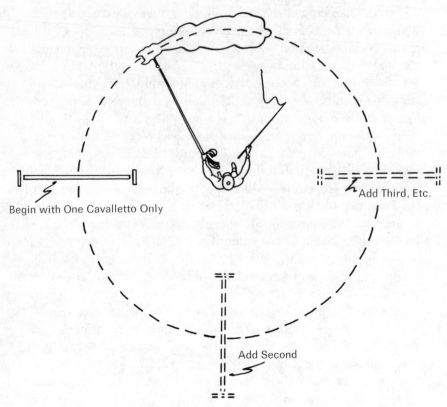

Fig. 86: Longeing circle with cavalletti used singly

the trot on the longe. The presentation is made first with a single bar on the ground, intersecting the circle. If the colt shows fear of it, he should be allowed to walk over it several times. Finally he must trot over it without hesitation with light encouragement of the whip if necessary. We now put four single bars on the circle as shown, until he trots calmly over them.

Now we begin to combine as shown. First two bars placed one meter twenty apart. Again, he may now need encouragement to place his trot step between them. Without rushing the process, we now increase by one until we finally have a maximum of five cavalletti as shown in fig. 87.

Work (at the trot only) should be done over these until the horse begins to cadence his trot. Over a period of time the cavalletti may be raised a little at a time until the tops are about six inches high. In response, the horse will begin to articulate higher and cadence.

We do not recommend that the horse under two years of age be worked at raised cavalletti. Up to this age the most that is desired is a free and normal trot without particular elevation. Collection is a desirable object *but it cannot be rushed* or you may achieve merely a false collection that consists mainly in over-flexion of the neck and a profile inside of the vertical.

It is natural for many young colts in action to elevate their

Fig. 87: Longeing circle with five cavalletti in line

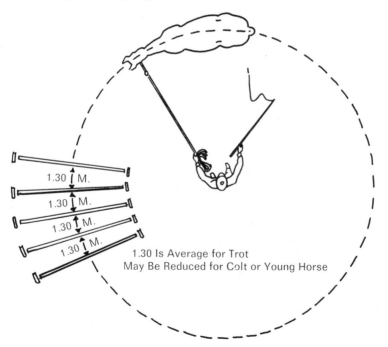

1.30 M.
1.30 M.
1.30 M.
1.30 M.

1.30 Is Average for Trot
May Be Reduced for Colt or Young Horse

muzzles and indulge in "star gazing." Only time and patience will gradually correct this, mainly by eventual use of the side reins.

When originally introduced they should be buckled to each side dee ring of the cavesson and each corresponding dee ring on the surcingle. They should be completely loose until the horse is well accustomed to them. They are progressively shortened over a long period of time until they finally come to exert a very slight elastic pull similar to the eventual rider's hands. Every care must be taken not to force the flexion of the young horse's neck, since we wish it to develop soft, flexible, and yielding. Tension and resistance in the muscles of the board of the neck are by all means to be avoided.

You will be put to some trouble in the use of the side reins. Every time you change direction you should readjust the lengths—the inside side rein always a little shorter than the outside. This will encourage a consistent curvature of the horse's dorsal spine from one end to the other and discourage him from everting his head outside the curvature.

We may now think of introducing the young horse to modest free jumping on the longe. As shown in fig. 88, this is best done on and off a straight bank of about two and a half feet. By moving the circle at will, the trainer presents the bank. The young horse may well need the encouragement of the longe whip under the hocks to jump up the first time, but he will quickly learn to jump on and jump off and enjoy the game.

We can now proceed to introduce him to as many varied shapes and colors as possible in order to make him bold. All obstacles should be *low* and easy for him to jump. We can combine colored bars, low chicken coops, and so forth. A line of colored balloons tied to a chicken coop is excellent, since it combines varied shapes, colors, and even motion.

If we assume that the horse is at least two and a half and reasonably strong in backbone, we can now consider the problem of getting him used to a rider on his back.

This process should not be rushed.

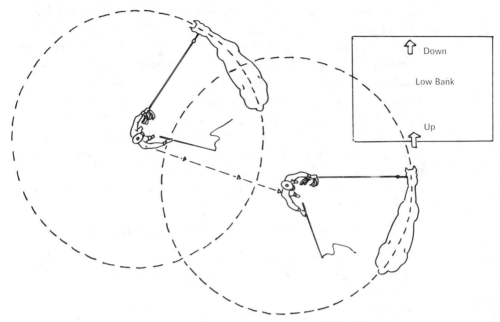

Fig. 88: Longeing circle moving to straight bank

The idea of "breaking" a horse to the rider is aptly termed. It implies "breaking" his spirit in a bucking contest, where, incidentally, the rider is quite apt to be humiliated by being unseated. The United States Plains Indians patiently "gentled" their horses until they were able to swing up with no objection on the part of the horse. They were among the great natural horsemen of history, able to ride horseback without bridle, or at the most a single line around the horse's nose. And they learned all these skills in only a few generations after their introduction to the horse.

The youngest colt during longeing can be taught to carry a saddle instead of the surcingle, so that we can assume that the two-year-old is accustomed to the saddle.

It is worthwhile to tie a forty-pound sandbag to the saddle and longe with it until the horse finds his balance. This can later be replaced with two forty-pound sandbags, equally balanced.

When the time comes to present the rider, do it gradually and with the lightest weight rider you can find. One hundred and ten pounds is a nice weight if you can find it. The rider is presented to the horse gradually, first merely approaching and leaning. The second stage is merely to put left foot in the stirrup while the horse stands. The third is to rise and lean the weight on the horse. None of these stages should be exceeded *until the horse accepts passively.* Finally, the rider is able to cross the leg over and settle down *softly* and *voluntarily.* He is now longed at all gaits with the horse. He has no reins. His progress will be directed by the trainer with the longe line.

F. RIDING THE HORSE INDEPENDENTLY

We now depart from the control of the longe. So far the line and whip have represented the eventual hands and legs of the rider. Now we make the transition with a soft noseband hackamore. There is nothing in the colt's mouth. He is receiving virtually the same pull on the cartilage of the nose from the reins of the hackamore as he received previously from the line and cavesson. Therefore this transition should be trauma-free for the horse.

With a lightweight rider he is thus ridden free. During this time we begin the transition from the voice, plus line and whip, to the physical aids, centered in the hands, legs, seat, and body weight of the rider. *This lightweight rider should be sensitive and capable!*

Properly managed with equestrian tact, over a period of a few weeks the horse makes the necessary transition by virtue of association. The knowing rider will constantly reinforce the physical aids with the voice commands the horse already understands.

We now think about bitting the horse. Again, *we proceed slowly!*

If you want a horse with a good mouth, use patience and it will be rewarded. Introduce the snaffle in the stall. Tie a small cheesecloth bag to the articulation with sugar in it. Let him wear it one hour per day as a *privilege!* The horse who clamps his jaws shut and raises his head to refuse the bit is a most disagreeable creature to deal with, and there is no necessity for this problem. After a few experiences of the sugar sensation, your horse will come after you, opening his mouth and begging for the snaffle. Once he is used to it, he can carry it on a headstall under the hackamore, *without reins*, and merely enjoy and mouth it.

Much complaint is heard in riding circles of horses with "mouths like iron." They are invariably made so by unknowledgeable or inconsiderate riders. Nature provided sensitive tissues originally. Treat and develop the mouth of your horse with patience and consideration and your reward will be a horse who is a joy to ride.

When our horse goes happily with snaffle and sugar without reins, we think about attaching them. *But we do not use them.* We use only the hackamore reins. Over a period of weeks, *little by little*, we begin to shorten the snaffle reins, until they are equal with length of hackamore reins. He is now on *both.* Just as gradually, over the next few weeks, we begin to lengthen the hackamore reins until we are on the snaffle.

Does this program seem long and painstaking? Perhaps. But it will give results. Shortcuts will mean going back and starting over, or possibly developing a hard-mouthed horse extremely unpleasant to ride.

We are now back to a previous chapter: Natural and Artificial Aids. So it is time to repeat: *"Never attempt to do with your reins what you can accomplish by your back, seat, legs, and body weight!"*

XII

Cavalletti

Proper use of the cavalletti is, of all schooling routines, the most useful and essential in preparing the horse for dressage, cross-country, or jumping.

It may, by proper spacing, be employed for the improvement of all three gaits.

A. PURPOSES

1. For the Horse

To achieve rhythmic cadence at the walk. To develop an articulated trot with elevation approaching the action of the passage. To improve the judgment of the horse in measuring his stride at the canter.

To enable the horse to learn how to properly use his back and neck.

To aid the strength of his muscular development.

To aid the elasticity of his muscular development.

To teach him to jump from the trot and so discourage "rushing."

2. For the Rider

To improve the rider's seat and sense of security.

To soften the articulation of the rider's waist.

To teach the rider how to accommodate to vertical displacement of the horse.

To teach the rider how to achieve independence of the hands, permitting consistent contact with the horse's mouth under all circumstances.

Finally, to teach the rider how to accommodate to the parabola of the jump off the trot with a measured, cadenced approach.

B. SPACING

Distances of cavalletti for the three gaits must be averaged. They may be somewhat varied for type of work desired and size and stride of the individual horse.

Fig. 89: Metal cavalletti stands

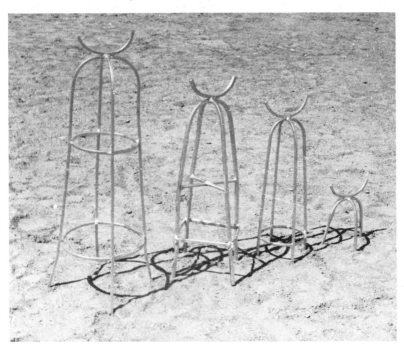

Spaced for the walk they should start at 80 cm and may open as much as 1.20 m for the extended walk.

Space for trot may begin at 1.20 m and open to 1.35 m.

Space for canter is 3.50 m (no stride). For one free stride of canter between cavalletti, distance is 7.20 m; for two free strides it is 10.50 m.

C. DIAMETER AND HEIGHTS

A proper cavalletto is a smooth wooden pole about three inches minimum diameter, preferably three meters long.

Usual height for walk and trot is six to eight inches overall.

Height for canter is 50 cm.

They may be held in place at the proper height by various simple devices.

Fig. 89 shows stands that we use at the Escuela for different heights. These are simply made of half-inch round or square metal rods.

Fig. 90 shows a ladderlike device of rails on which five cavalletti can be quickly assembled.

Fig. 90: Rails with cavalletti

Fig. 91: Rider at cavalletti—erect seat

D. METHODS OF WORK

In introducing the horse to cavalletti at any gait, he should at first be presented only *one at a time!*

This has been suggested in the section on longeing.

Only when the horse navigates one cavalletto without breaking stride should he be given two. This is gradually increased to a maximum of five cavalletti in a row, never more.

Some of the exercises for horse and rider at cavalletti that have been found useful here at the Escuela are as follows:

1. Riders come through cavalletti at trot, sitting vertical with soft waist, light contact with horse's mouth, looking straight ahead, impulsing with legs as necessary (fig. 91).

2. Riders come through as above but without stirrups (fig. 92).

3. Riders come through with stirrups, inclined forward at the waist, hands wide apart but in contact with horse's mouth, looking straight ahead.

Fig. 92: Rider at cavalletti—erect seat, no stirrups

Fig. 93: Rider at cavalletti flexed forward, hands apart

Fig. 94: Riders at cavalletti in pair, holding hands

Fig. 95: Riders at cavalletti in pair, hands to each other's shoulders

Fig. 96: Rider jumps figure X from cavalletti

4. Riders come through in pairs holding hands (fig. 94).

5. Riders come through in pairs with hands on each other's shoulders (fig. 95).

6. An extremely low figure-X bar is placed 3.50 m from last cavalletti (fig. 96).

7. This figure-X is replaced by single bar 50 cm high (fig. 97).

8. Obstacle is gradually built to a triple bar (never higher than four feet) to be jumped from the trot (fig. 98).

Combining Trot with Canter

Trotting cavalletti may be at center of arena. On one major side, place three cavalletti for canter (3.50 m) at maximum height of 50 cm. Riders come through center at trot, initiating canter after turning on to the major side.

Riders may come through cantering cavalletti first in normal position, with stirrups and reins (fig. 99).

They can then be asked to knot the reins and come through

Fig. 97: Rider jumps single bar from cavalletti

Fig. 98: Rider jumps triple bar (no higher than four feet) from cavalletti

Fig. 99: Rider at canter cavalletti

with arms extended (fig. 100).

    They may also come through with hands on hips (fig. 101).

    When sufficiently adept, they can come through without stirrups and hands on hips or extended (fig. 102).

Fig. 100: Rider at canter cavalletti, reins knotted, arms extended

Fig. 101: Rider at canter cavalletti, reins knotted, hands on hips

Fig. 102: Rider at canter cavalletti, reins knotted, no stirrups.

XIII

Gaits

A. THE THREE GAITS

We recognize three *natural* gaits of the horse: the walk, trot, and canter.

It is worth noting that the actual mechanics of these gaits evaded human understanding until the close of the nineteenth century. In 1898 Eadweard Muybridge published his monumental work *Animals in Motion*, made possible by the early resources of photography and the dedicated genius of a great scientific mind.

It was a controversy of the early 1870's that stimulated Muybridge to undertake his investigations. The controversy involved the mechanics of the horse's trot. One group claimed that at one phase of the trot all four members were off the ground. Another group maintained the contrary. Naturally, Muybridge's research finally proved incontrovertibly that *a period of suspension*, when all four limbs were off the ground, existed in the mechanics of both the trot and the canter.

1. The Phases of Each Gait

In riding practice we recognize three phases of each gait:
a. Ordinary

b. Strong or extended

c. Collected

In the ordinary phase of the gait, the horse moves his legs in *natural* extension.

In the extended phase of the gait both hinds and forelegs are pushed forward and each stride is longer. In those gaits with a period of suspension (all members off the ground), that period of suspension will be longer.

In the collected phase, stride will be shorter, and much of the forward motion will be converted to vertical articulation.

The center of gravity of the horse varies in motion between the fourteenth and seventeenth vertebrate. It will be farthest forward in the extended phases of the gaits and farthest back at the collected, thus demanding a compensation in the angle of the rider's upper body, which will be near vertical at collection and inclined well forward at extension.

2. How the Beginning Rider May Come To Distinguish Among the Three Phases of Each Gait

The rider may start at any given letter in the arena, making a complete circuit at what he believes to be the ordinary phase of any gait. He will now count strides. He now repeats, attempting to extend the gait. There should be considerably fewer strides counted if the horse has truly extended, since each stride is longer. We now repeat at the collected phase. This should involve many *more* counted strides than the ordinary.

B. THE WALK

This is a four-beat rhythm in which the horse invariably leads with one hind. A typical progression is: (1) left hind, (2) left fore, (3) right hind, (4) right fore.

Of the three gaits, the walk is the most difficult to extend and collect, having less flexibility than the other two gaits. Major movement will be found to be more in the head and neck than in the back of the horse.

Each gait has its own type of displacement to which the rider must accommodate. Because of the reaction of the head and neck noted above, the displacement of the walk is largely in a horizontal plane, with a minimum of vertical elevation. This accommodation demands that the rider develop a loosely articulated waist, which will yield to a forward-backward displacement, keeping the upper body relatively stable. If constant contact with the mouth is to be maintained, the hands too must follow in a horizontal plane, giving and taking. Both of these demands will be increased as the walk begins to extend.

1. Ordinary Walk

The ordinary walk, executed correctly, implies some impulsion on the part of the rider. The horse must indulge in deliberate action, *not an aimless shuffle!* His hinds should print directly in the track of the fores, both in straight lines and in curves. If the horse responds satisfactorily to the initial impulse of the rider's legs, the aids may then be kept passive except to initiate turns.

2. Extended Walk

To achieve this air the rider must use not only the legs as an impulsor force but the lower back as well. He must induce the horse to extend the neck and seek the support of the rider's hands, which must follow in a horizontal plane. The legs should be used *alternately.* As the left forehand *initiates* its forward progress, the left leg should be applied to lengthen that *step.* When the left fore is about to print it is too late to influence it. (Remember that a step is merely one section or phase of a complete stride sequence.) When the right forehand begins to move, the right leg should be applied. This is accompanied by the bracing of the lower back as an impulsor force. The result is that the horse gradually increases the reach of the individual steps, resulting in a longer stride. The more the horse is induced to extend, *the more support he will need from the rider's hand.* As extension increases, the prints of the hinds will begin to reach ahead of the prints of the forehand. This overprint may reach as much as thirteen inches in the case of some horses.

3. Collected Walk

This air, again, requires *impulse.* It is not a shuffle. The position of the rider is vertical, and initially, at least, his center of gravity will be behind that of the horse, inducing him to "come back to him." Again, the legs are used alternately, together with the back as a strong impulsor. But now the hands act *alternately,* shortening the step of each forehand. As a result, forward motion will begin to translate into vertical articulation. The accordion of the horse's body will begin to close in collection. His quarters will begin to come under his mass, aiding impulsion. His head and neck will rise and his profile come in to the vertical (never beyond).

C. THE TROT

The trot is a two-beat rhythm in which each pair of *diagonal* feet is alternately lifted and advanced in unison. The body of the horse makes a transit forward twice during each complete stride, without support. In other words there are, in each stride of the trot, two phases in which all four members of the horse are off the ground.

The displacement of the horse at the trot is largely vertical. The accommodation of the rider to this displacement at the sitting trot is described in Chapter V, The Seat of the Mounted Rider. The other accommodation is the action of posting in the rising trot.

1. Ordinary Trot Sitting

Seat of the rider is maintained by making upper back convex when horse is dropping out and concave when horse is rising. *Not too much weight must be put in the stirrups or depth of seat will be lost.* Aids for impulsion are similar to the walk, but legs may now be used in unison rather than alternately.

2.   Ordinary Trot Posting

To maintain the impulsion of the ordinary trot posting, the legs of the rider will close simultaneously on the horse, in cadence with the stride, only when the horse seems to be in danger of losing impulsion. The lower back too, of course, does its part as an impulsor force. The upper body of the rider, which was close to the vertical at the sitting trot, is now inclined well forward. In order to produce the leverage necessary for the rider to rise easily at the post *the lower legs must be well back of the girth and the heels down.* This enables the rider to push down in the heel at each rise, utilizing the base of the stirrup as a platform. Fig. 103 shows correct and incorrect position of the lower leg for posting. The rider with lower leg too far forward suffers two difficulties. He must expend far too much effort to rise and he will be constantly behind the action of the horse, because he is behind his own center of gravity.

The action of the rising trot implies the lifting of the rider's pelvic region *only.* There should be no vertical movement of the shoulders. As the sitting bones leave the seat, the pelvis is thrust upward and forward in an easy and rhythmic motion. The seat should rise vertically only to the minimum amount necessary to clear the action of the horse. Its forward motion will not be absolutely straight forward, but lightly oriented toward the diagonal on which one is posting.

When riding in the exterior there is of course no inside or outside diagonal, only a left and right. When you are posting for long periods the diagonal should be changed regularly so that the horse's muscular development will be consistent. Constantly posting on one preferred pair of diagonals will highly develop musculature on those diagonals only and leave the other pair much less developed.

Fig. 103: Correct (top) and incorrect position (bottom) of the lower
leg at posting trot

In order to change diagonals the posting rider must either sit a half beat or elevate a half beat. He will then automatically be thrust onto the opposite pair of diagonals.

3. Collected Trot (Always Sitting)

Impulsor legs are applied *more* vigorously, well behind the girth, to both impulse and to bring the hocks of the horse in under his mass. Upper body of the rider is at the vertical with seat well down in the deepest part of the saddle. As the haunches come under, the neck of the horse will rise and develop curvature. The profile of the face begins to approach the vertical. The fingers or wrists act alternately on the reins to shorten stride, again converting much of the forward motion into vertical articulation. Merely a slow trot is not a collected trot. It is only collected if the body of the horse is sufficiently compacted.

4. Extended Trot (Posting)

Since the extended trot sitting is only asked for at the highest levels of international competition, we will here confine ourselves to the extended trot posting. It should be borne in mind that the fully extended trot, especially on a large horse of high vertical displacement, makes inordinate demands on the accommodation of the rider who is seated. All of the displacement must be taken up in the rider's back and waist articulation.

To develop the extended trot posting, at least while schooling, it will be found helpful to separate the hands out to the level of the knees and drop them down to knee level. As the horse extends the neck to reach for the bit, the rider must "take hold" and give support. Legs and lower back urge the horse forward as the support of the hand is increased. When certain of support, the horse will begin to reach out and increase stride. Full extension implies that the horse extends the forelegs with no bend whatever at the knee joint.

D. THE CANTER

A three-beat gait in which horse advances with one pair
of laterals in advance of the other pair. If the left pair is leading, he is said to be on the left lead, and vice versa. The complete stride includes one period of suspension when all members
are off the ground.

The displacement of the canter is unlike that of either the
walk or the trot. It can best be described as a rocking motion
felt at both extremes of an arc. Therefore the accommodation
of the rider to this displacement consists in thrusting forward
and backward with the pelvic region in order to maintain
contact with the seat. The action required is almost identical
with that one uses in a swing, thrusting forward with the lower
back when the swing is in upward transit and receiving when it
returns. When sitting the canter properly one should have no
difficulty maintaining a dollar bill in place between seat and
saddle.

Riding the arena on the left hand or in any curvature to the
left, the horse if at canter is expected to be on the left lead.
This puts the inside hind under him at the turns, and since he
is canted to the inside it acts as a post of support. Should he
be turning at the canter on the false lead, he has no inside rear
base of support and is in danger of falling. Exception is the
counter-canter as described under 4.

1. Ordinary Canter

The horse is put to the canter by either lateral or diagonal
aids as described in Chapter VI, Natural and Artificial Aids.
The rider *sits* this canter and accommodates to the displacement as described above. The upper body of the rider will be
inclined moderately forward. In cantering on the left lead, the
weight will be in the left stirrup with left leg at the girth.
Weight will be on the left sitting bone. Right leg will be well
behind the girth. Whenever the horse shows of breaking back
to the trot, the right leg must act to prevent this. The horse

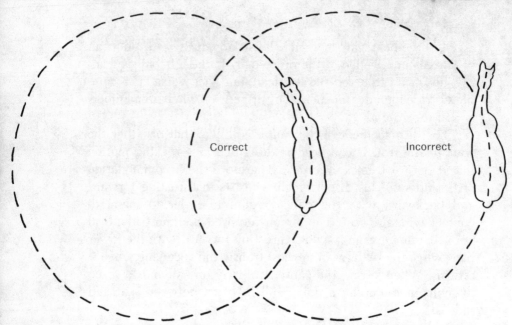

Correct   Incorrect

Fig. 104: Curvature of horse's spine at canter on the curved line

should be kept on light support of the hands with major
tension in the left or leading hand, which, in schooling at least,
is best carried *lower* than the off hand by about the height of
a fist.

In cantering turns or circular figures make certain that you
can see the inside eye and inside nostril of your horse. This
will insure the correct location of his head. On curved figures
there must be a constant curvature of the horse's dorsal spine
from poll to dock. Fig. 104 shows correct and incorrect curvature of the horse when cantering curved figures.

2. Collected Canter

The description given for the ordinary canter applies to
the collected canter with the following exceptions: At the collected canter the upper body of the rider will be *vertical*. The
weight will be down into the deepest part of the saddle. Since

the center of gravity of the rider is further back than it is if upper body is inclined forward, the horse is induced to shorten stride. He is further induced toward this by the deterrent action of the hands. In cantering on the left lead, the fingers of left hand should close as deterrent at the time the left pair of laterals begins its transit. This should be followed by the fingers of the right hand, influencing the opposite pair of laterals. *Strong impulsion must be maintained.*

3. Extended Canter

Again, the description given for the ordinary canter applies with the following exceptions: The upper body of the rider will now incline far forward as described in Chapter VI as the "light seat." Although the rider is still seated, sending the center of gravity that far forward will induce the horse to lengthen stride considerably.

For the most speed and fullest extension of the canter, the rider leaves the saddle and adopts the "forward seat" as described in Chapter VI. Appropriate use of leg and crop, if necessary, will cause the horse to "flat out," cantering at maximum extension. This is the "cross-country" seat, also appropriate for hunting when hounds are chasing. *It is not the seat with which to approach fences, however!*

4. The Counter-canter

Properly a dressage maneuver, it may be best clarified in this context. As dressage schooling advances and the balance of the horse improves, he can be taught to balance himself in curvature on the false lead, which is referred to as the counter-canter. The best way of initiating this is from the semi-volte at the canter. After completing the semi-volte, continue at the canter around the arena without permitting the horse to change leads.

With a sensitive horse, particularly, this requires great tact and control of body weight on the part of the rider. The active leg, which has now become the *inside* leg, must be kept in constant contact behind the girth as a reminder to the horse that he is not to change leads. Even a slight weight shift to the inside on the part of the rider may cause the horse to make a flying change in order to find the support he is accustomed to.

Only when your horse is executing this satifactorily, should you proceed to the next step, which should be *large* figure eights, preventing your horse from changing leads as you initiate the second circle.

Once adept at this you may attempt to initiate a circle at the counter-canter.

5. Cross-Canter

Should the horse be found to be leading with right forefoot and left hind, or vice versa, he will be disunited and is in danger of falling on the turns. He should immediately be interrupted and put again to the canter.

XIV

Jumping

A. BACKGROUND OF STADIUM JUMPING

The jumping of stadium obstacles has a far briefer history than have other aspects of the equestrian art. Before the turn of the present century, jumping was limited to the rustic obstacles encountered in the hunt and in point-to-point races.

Show jumping was not included in the Olympic Games until 1912. As of the present, this phase of horsemanship seems to be growing in popularity on a worldwide basis faster than any other aspect of the sport.

There is of course more than one approach to the technique of jumping. It should be emphasized, however, that the essential differences between the equestrian teams of the various nations are minimal. There is, for example, far less difference between the technique employed by the United States Equestrian Team and the teams of France, England, and Germany than there is between the United States team and a large proportion of popular U.S. open jumping. Since the teams of the various nations represent their nations' greatest potential in Olympic competition, it is reasonable to assume that their techniques and approach will offer them the greatest chance for success.

The approach of the Escuela Ecuestre to jumping is essentially the international approach, with certain typically Mexican accents. These latter were developed by Mexico's team during the 1940s and 1950s when Mexico achieved the remarkable record of winning the Nation's Cup in international jumping eighteen out of twenty consecutive years.

The most rhythmic concept of the jump is achieved by considering it not as an isolated phenomenon but as merely one stride of the canter which is higher and longer than preceding or succeeding strides. Although all stadium jumping is done from the canter, practice jumping is often done from the trot, or even walk, in order to school both horse and rider. Jumping off the trot enables us to use cavalletti in front of the fence and thereby cadence the approach of the horse. The horse that can jump four feet from the trot can naturally jump considerably higher from the canter where the launching force is proportionally greater. As far as the rider is concerned, the accommodation demanded in jumping from the trot is far greater than from the canter over the same fence, since the parabola from the trot is shorter.

Experience teaches us that the extent of instruction possible during actual jumping sessions is completely inadequate unless preceded by thorough theory orientation in the classroom. The complete sequence of the jump occurs rapidly and permits the instructor to yell only a relatively few words of advice. Given the preoccupation of the rider with his mount and the problems at hand, sometimes even these few words fail to get his attention.

It now becomes obvious, therefore, that in addition to theory inculcation, means must be found to divide the act of jumping into its component segments and for purposes of schooling put it into divided slow motion. Here at the Escuela Ecuestre we initiate this by jumping up onto three-foot straight banks. During this process we are able to criticize and improve what constitutes phase one of the three phases of the parabola. Jumping off the same bank will simulate phase three, or landing

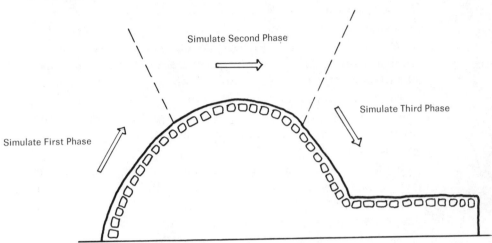

Fig. 105: Mound with banks

phase, and permit the same criticism.

Another means is the mound with banks which we have constructed and illustrated in the accompanying drawing (fig. 105). As shown in the illustration, this enables the instructor to criticize all three phases of the parabola in relation to the position of the rider.

B. THE ACTUAL JUMP

In its complete sequence, the jump is divided into the following phases:

1. **Approach**

2. **First phase**

3. **Second phase**

4. **Third phase**

5. Departure

Given the above analysis, inevitably the art of conduction is implied. This simply means that one *conducts* the horse in such a manner that the various jumps presented become easier for the horse to accomplish, rather than more difficult. Conduction through a pre-set course or series of obstacles is merely a further complication or amplification of the problem that exists in the proper conduction of a horse through even one practice obstacle.

Proper conduction through the sequence of even one practice obstacle is primarily dependent on the line of sight and visual orientation of the rider. Let us assume an approach at the canter to an obstacle which is at our right hand. When we pass the obstacle at our right, we must direct our vision at the obstacle so that our turn to the right will be properly made. The proper turn will place the horse at 90 degrees to the frontage of the fence. Should we fail to keep the obstacle under constant visual surveillance, the arc of approach may very well put us at an angle to approach that may invite the horse to run out on either hand by either making the arc of approach to wide or too narrow.

It is well to remember the problem of the fence as the horse sees it. In passing the fence that we must turn into and approach, we know our intention, but the horse does not. Only at the moment of commitment at 90 degrees to the frontage does the horse understand what is being asked of him. It is at precisely this moment that he must make a series of complicated calculations and come up with an instantaneous answer. The factors consist of complex variables similar to computer data; among them are such factors as the horse's own size and power potential, the weight of his rider, the distance to the obstacle, the length of the last few strides in order to achieve proper placement for takeoff, the height of the obstacle, the width of the obstacle, and the form of the desired parabola. We can add to this the fact that at the point of takeoff equine vision is such that the horse can no longer see the part of the obstacle he must jump but only the extreme left and right.

The equine calculator is so constituted that the horse is able to make these calculations, come up with an instantaneous answer, depart, and take the obstacle, usually successfully.

Now let us return to the problem of conduction on the part of the rider. Once committed at 90 degrees to the obstacle, there must be no psychological or physical hesitation on the part of the rider, or the horse will instantly sense it. Entrance must be made with confidence, courage, and determination.

The position and center of gravity of the rider will be largely determined by his line of sight. Up until commitment, eyes are directed at the obstacle for the purpose of placement. Now the vision should be directed *above* the obstacle or at the next obstacle if one exists. The fence remains in the peripheral vision of the rider. Any attempt to keep it in the primary vision inevitably leads to a lowering of the head, rounding of the upper back and shift of the center of gravity forward at the very time that this shift will inhibit the lifting of the forehand of the horse in the first phase. Very often this unfortunate shift is accompanied by an involuntary raising of the hands which pull on the mouth of the horse, thus distracting or disturbing him.

The problem of conduction naturally becomes·more complex when a series of fences or course of obstacles is involved. We are now concerned with the problem of control of velocity and changes of leads. Except for obstacle number one, where the rider is permitted to circle on either lead for entry, the course designer determines on which lead we shall enter most obstacles if they involve other than a straight line approach from a previous fence.

It is well to remember that under most circumstances a horse approaching an obstacle on the right lead will land on the left and vice versa. If we therefore assume that obstacle number two is on the right lead, then we should opt to circle on the left lead before number one, thus placing ourselves on the correct lead for number two with no loss of time. If by course design we are forced to land on the left lead when the right lead is indicated for the next fence, then a change of lead on landing is essential. This is usually achieved by means of a half halt, at which time the opposite diagonal aids are applied. The so-called flying change is usually employed only when a form of the figure-S is involved. It *is* possible to cause the horse to change leads while in the second phase of the parabola over the fence. It requires excellent timing and advanced equestrian tact. When a horse is completely airborne he may well react to lighter aids than when earthbound. Therefore, if one is at the second phase (when the horse is horizontal to the ground), having approached on the right lead, one may put weight in the right stirrup, call slightly with the right hand, and touch behind the girth with the left leg. The horse responds by changing leads mid-air, thus landing on the right lead instead of the left.

Velocity, and its control, is the other major concern in taking a course of obstacles. Normal velocity for a jumping course is 350 meters per minute. Obviously one must come in initially with enough impulse and velocity to facilitate jumping. However, it is the tendency of many eager jumping horses to increase velocity after each fence. If unchecked, such a horse may easily increase velocity after five or six fences to 500 or more meters per minute. This will usually result in a loss of collection and eventually lead either to a runout or a crash.

Checking of velocity is usually done by the half halt. This employs all the aids to the halt but sends the horse forward immediately. He is thus forced to take up a new cadence and a new velocity. Most often the physical aids are reinforced by the voice so that on the jumping field one seldom hears the voice urging the horse on, but on the contrary, constant verbal commands to the halt in order to aid checking.

Previously we have mentioned the problem of circling in front of fence number one. This involves the general theory of circling in front of any fence for approach. Figure 106 shows that the circle in front of the fence *must* be based

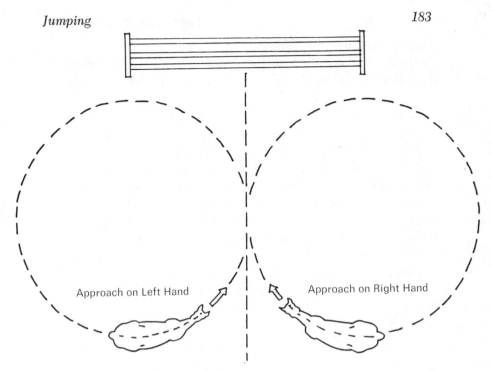

Approach on Left Hand

Approach on Right Hand

Fig. 106: Tangent is 90 degrees to center of frontage
Same pattern for figure eight

on a tangent 90 degrees to the frontage. This tangent permits a circle to either side or combining the two into a figure-eight for schooling and correction of vices.

This device is used both for the refuser and for the rusher. The refuser will tend to brace himself for refusal at the time he reaches the tangent and faces the fence. When he has been circled or figure-eighted enough times, he will become convinced that he is not to be asked to take the fence. When the horse finally faces the fence without breaking stride, the rider puts in the aids strongly and the horse takes the fence before he has time to prepare refusal.

Conversely, the rusher will prepare his rush at exactly the same point of the tangent to the circle. When he is taken out enough times he too will become convinced that no jump is involved. When the aids are finally applied, unable to prepare his rush he will go in cadence to the fence.

Following is an analysis of the five elements of jumping, including the three phases of the jump itself.

1. Approach

a. Approach should be *collected* for all elements of height. The horse that is heavy on the forehand does not have his haunches under him and therefore has relatively little ability to jump high. By far the most difficult fence to navigate is a simple straight vertical, since there are no preliminary bars to suggest the parabola. Approach for the broad jump (water obstacle, etc.) may be more extended and suggest increased velocity, since the parabola is longer and lower. The problem of a broad jump before a difficult element of height is particularly a challenge, since it involves extending the horse for the broad jump and immediately collecting him for the height which follows. This was well illustrated in the final day of the 1968 Olympics in Mexico where an Olympic water jump of

Fig. 107 : Seat of rider during

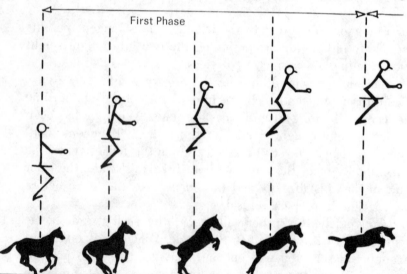

First Phase

seventeen feet was followed by a hazardous double fence.

b. The horse may be checked and collected, but the velocity of the last few strides before the fence should be properly left to his own judgment. Obviously a small horse will need greater velocity than a big long Thoroughbred in order to get over the same fence.

c. The rider should be *seated* on approach, driving with seat and back to control and stabilize the haunches of the horse. Only the seated rider has sufficient base of support to have complete freedom of the use of his impulsor legs. Anticipation by going forward *before* the fence serves to move the center of gravity of the rider forward over the very portion of the horse that must rise, namely, the forehand. This is in violation of all known mechanical precepts of similar conditions. If a pilot wishes to gain altitude his controls are designed to enable him to lighten the nose of the ship, which must rise first. If at the moment of attempting to raise his plane, all baggage and passengers were moved to the cockpit, the change in center of

the entire jumping sequence

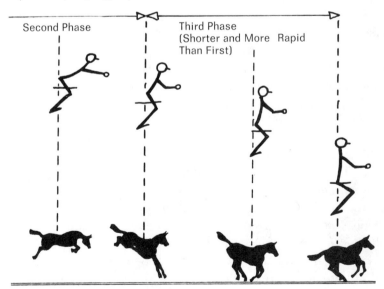

Second Phase

Third Phase
(Shorter and More Rapid
Than First)

gravity would make his task difficult indeed.

d. Legs should close on the horse in cadence several strides before the fence. Both legs should be applied vigorously behind the girth as impulsors just before the fence.

e. Hands: The horse is held on light support of the hand on all of the approach. Never abandon the horse by throwing him away in front of the fence. The horse that jumps between the hands and legs is designed to carry a rider. The horse taught to jump on a loose rein is designed to carry a passenger.

It is true that during schooling sessions we ask students to tie off the reins and go through low obstacles without reins or stirrups. The very purpose of these exercises is to establish *independent equilibrium of the rider* so that he will not look to the reins to support himself. This equilibrium establishes the independence of the hand in giving and taking rein during the jump.

2. **Phase One** (**See Fig. 107 for phases 1, 2, and 3.**)

a. The *seated* rider leaves the forehand of the horse free to rise, at the same time stabilizing the haunches from which motive power is derived.

b. The rider, being flexible, allows the impetus of the horse to thrust him forward, flexing at the waist. This is not a *voluntary* action but more accurately a flexible *reaction*.

c. As the hinge of the waist is closing, the hinge of the elbows is opening. The combination of these two factors enables the rider to give rein as the initial extension of the head and neck of the horse requires.

3. **Phase Two** (**Fig. 108.**)

a. In this phase the horse is horizontal to the ground and midway over the obstacle. He has now achieved maximum extension of head and neck and will therefore require maximum cession of rein by the rider. *The contact of the rider's hands with the mouth of the horse should be maintained.*

b. At this point the rider's seat will be out of the saddle to the *minimum* required, depending on the height of the jump

Fig. 108: Excellent seat of mounted rider in phase 2 of jump (Cap. Roger Barceló, Cab. Mexicana)

and the parabola of the horse. The rider will now have attained maximum waist flexion. His vision will be straight ahead, *not looking down*. The ability of the rider to go forward at the waist (deforming) is dependent on the quality of flexibility. The ability of the rider to recover, or reform, is dependent on the quality of elasticity.

c. The rider is now preparing for the next stage by putting his weight down on his heels by ankle flexion in order to take up the shock of landing.

4. Phase Three

a. When the horse begins his descent, the rider begins his recovery. As previously stated, recovery is dependent on the quality of elasticity. The impulse to recover initiates from the shoulders, *not* from the back. The initial act of recovery is the opening of the shoulders and therefore recovery with a *concave* back rather than convex.

b. As the horse descends, his head and neck begin to *elevate*. The rider now begins to take back rein to the extent that the horse yields it. The hinge of the waist is now *opening* and the hinge of the elbows *closing*.

c. After landing on the forehand, the horse lands on his hinds, at which point the forehand elevates. Here it is essential that the rider be fully seated in order to urge the horse forward in the desired direction. The shock of landing in terms of the rider is divided between three springs: the flexed ankle, the hinge of the knee, and the hinge of the hip.

5. Departure

a. The impulse for departure will depend on whether it is desirable to go straight forward, right or left, or whether a change of lead is necessary.

C. DISOBEDIENCE—CAUSES, AND METHODS OF CORRECTION

1. Runout

Most frequent cause is failure of rider to come at right angles to the obstacle on center. The diagonal approach invites the runout. Another cause may be the memory of the horse of a mishap at the same obstacle. In this case the obstacle should be made easy for him, to rebuild his confidence. A third cause may be lack of collection. If the horse is disarticulated and heavy on the forehand, he may sense his inability to jump. The runout may be prevented by relatively simple means. An understanding of equine psychology indicates that a horse, once having run out or shown a tendency to run out to the left, will continue to attempt his runout on the *same* side. He does not confound his rider by running out first to the left and then to the right, or vice versa. The provident rider can therefore prevent subsequent runouts by the following means: Runout to the left—carry the left rein higher than the right, close to the horse's neck, forming a left barrier for the forehand. Exert more pressure with the left leg *behind the girth* than with the right, thus forming a left barrier for the quarters. On approaching the fence exert a series of calls of the fingers of the *right* hand, thus calling the mouth of the horse to the right. Runout to the right—the same procedure in reverse.

2. Refusal

Most frequent cause is lack of impulsion on the part of the rider (i.e., failure of legs and lower back of rider as impulsors). Another frequent cause is lack of determination and moral courage on the part of the rider. This is instantly sensed by the horse and diminishes his own determination.

3. Collision

Usually occurs because the horse is out of cadence or off stride. This is closely related to common problems of jumpers— the horse that will not stand off his fences and the horse that launches his parabola from too far away. Both of these habits may be corrected in schooling by use of a take-off bar. In the case of the horse that will not stand off, the take-off bar is placed either on the ground or slightly raised at the normal point of take-off, thus forcing the horse to stand off a normal distance. In the case of the opposite fault, the take-off bar is raised to the level of a low obstacle, placed far enough in front of the primary obstacle so that on landing from the first bar the horse is forced to jump the primary obstacle with no intervening stride.

Show jumping is an extremely demanding sport. It requires courage, patience, discipline, and great physical coordination. It also demands a sympathetic understanding of your horse's psychology and physical capabilities. The rewards are great. Many consider it the most exhilarating sport in which humans are privileged to indulge.

XV

Dressage—High School

Some explanation of dressage at the *haute école* level is in order, for there seems to exist in certain riding circles some misunderstanding of the term and its implications. It is not an esoteric equine ritual to which certain buffs are addicted.

The term dressage derives from the French verb *dresser*, which simply means "to train."

The fact that you teach your horse the maneuvers here described does not necessarily imply that you wish to enter dressage competitions. It does imply that you wish to derive the most pleasure and satisfaction out of your riding by having a strong, supple, and capable horse, responsive and obedient to your aids. The rewards that will be yours cannot be overestimated or properly described. One has to experience them firsthand to appreciate them. You and your horse will embark on a joint venture together that, with mutual tolerance and understanding, will bring great rewards to both of you.

It used to be the belief of gentlemen hunters and jumpers of the "old school" that "dressage" was about the worst form of schooling a jumping horse could be put to. They looked upon collection as a jumper's vice. Experience in the modern equestrian world has, of course, proved this assumption completely fallacious.

I recall being at Madison Square Garden in 1963 for the

international jumping events. It was a year in which the West German jumping team appeared with really enormous horses and successfully flattened all opposition. What amazed me was the agility and handiness of these big, heavy horses, obviously carrying much blood of the German coach horse. When I asked a young German team rider about their schooling methods, he answered me very simply: "Dressage, dressage, and more dressage!"

A. PURPOSE

The purpose of any dressage is to make the horse flexible, obedient, and strong. At the same time it serves to train the rider by making him sensitive to the movements of the horse under him and makes him learn to balance his aids.

From the standpoint of the rider there are three essentials to the practice of dressage. First he must learn to *feel* what the horse is doing under him. Then he must learn to *interpret* what he feels. Then he must learn to *influence* the horse.

The horse must learn to respond to the directions given by the rider through his aids. He must be developed muscularly so that he can bend his whole body in the pattern of the movement, move any of his four legs in a given direction, at the request of the rider, and increase or decrease the length of his stride at all gaits, at the request of the rider.

B. MOVEMENTS

All dressage movements are based upon *natural* movements of the horse. This even includes the "above-the-ground airs" as taught in the Spanish School in Vienna. We are discussing the controlled perfection of various movements that at one time or another the horse may do of his own accord in the free state. They are not to be confused with tricks or so-called circus airs.

The order in which the following movements are given is

the order in which they should be taught to the horse. They progress logically from the easier to the more difficult. With patience and understanding on the part of the rider, the horse will progress. His normal attention span should not be exceeded by demands he cannot yet meet physically. He should not be permitted to become bored, sour, and thus recalcitrant. If he finds great difficulty learning a new exercise, go back to one he *can* do so that you can justly praise him and he can go back to the barn feeling like a success. If he goes back disgraced, feeling like a failure, your work the next day will be that much more difficult. *A horse thrives on praise!*

1. Turn on the Forehand

Purpose is to mobilize the horse's hind quarters so that he will take one or more steps with just his hind quarters in the direction the rider desires and on command. This is initiated on the track at the wall and is therefore a half turn on the forehand. A half turn on the forehand to the left means quarters to the right.

In the half turn on the forehand to the left, the rider first collects the horse, sits *vertical* with weight on right sitting bone. Left leg is applied behind the girth until the horse takes *one* step with quarters to the right. The leg is instantly relaxed. The leg is then reapplied to command a second step. The right or passive leg is held at the girth ready to act should the horse take more than one step or step too fast. The rider's hands hold the horse on the bit and prevent forward motion. If the horse is extremely slow to respond with quarters to the right, the rider may increase tension on the left rein, turning head slightly to the left. If, on the contrary, there is an overresponse, the head should be turned slightly to the right.

Fig. 109 shows that in quarters to the right the horse is using his right front foot as a pivot that is picked up and put down in place. The left foot walks a small half circle around it. Usually three steps are enough to turn the horse 90 degrees and six steps to reach 180 degrees.

The horse should not be allowed to step of his own accord,

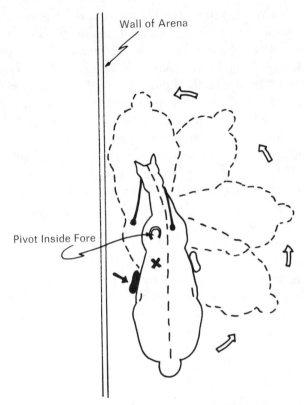

Wall of Arena

Pivot Inside Fore

Fig. 109: Half turn on forehand to left

but only on command of the leg. The maneuver should be in a cadenced rhythm that becomes eccentric when the horse steps voluntarily. The interval of time between applications of the leg may be gradually reduced until the horse appears to be in continuous cadenced motion.

2.   Reinback

The purpose of the reinback is to teach the horse to move backward at the walk as readily, gracefully, and obediently as he does forward. Again, the rider must first collect the horse. The aids can be considered lateral, since the left hand is used with the left leg and the right hand with the right leg.

Rider carries his shoulders slightly back of the vertical with lower legs close to horse's sides. Tightening the fingers of the right hand is accompanied by pushing backward with the right leg. As the horse yields he takes half a step backward with the right foreleg. Immediately the tension of the right hand and leg is relaxed and the tension begins with left hand and left leg until horse yields with a half step with left foreleg. Each step back is therefore made up of two phases.

Legs are held in readiness to correct displacement of the haunch. If the haunch displaces to the right, the rider promptly presses right leg firmly behind the girth and turns head of horse slightly to the right with indirect rein thereby opposing lateral movement of haunch with forehand.

The reinback requires that the horse be held between the hands and legs of the rider. The hand and leg of the rider on each side may be considered the extremes of two imaginary shafts that form a barrier on each side of the horse, preventing lateral displacement. The cadence of the walk at the reinback should be just as even and measured as the walk forward.

3. Straight Line Forward

The same two imaginary shafts referred to above control the straight line forward, usually practiced on the medium line A-C, away from the wall. After turning at A, the horse is sent forward in a straight line whether at walk, trot, or canter. If the rider truly has the horse between the hands and legs and is sufficiently experienced at *feeling, interpreting,* and *influencing* the horse, the latter will actually advance on a straight path, the prints of the hinds following exactly in the track of the forehand. Seen from the front there will be no visible wobbling to the sides.

4. The Halt

Contrary to what many people think, the horse is not correctly halted by simply pulling on the reins. Even when it is possible to do so, the horse so halted will be found to be standing unbalanced, with the major weight on his forehand. He is thus unable to move forward smoothly on command, as he would be if halted collected.

Aids

There are two correct methods of using the hand in the halt: (1) on the active hand, and (2) on the fixed hand. In both methods the use of the legs and back is identical. The less-experienced rider should use the active hand. The fixed hand is a more sophisticated method and requires some practice to develop.

With the horse in forward motion at any gait, the rider sets his shoulders slightly behind the vertical and closes both legs on the horse, *well behind the girth.* Using the closed legs as leverage, he braces the lower back and *deepens his seat.* The immediate effect of this, if the hands were not used, would be to make the horse go faster. However, the hands are actively used (two direct reins of opposition), not in a steady pull, but increasing and decreasing tension in cadence with each stride, until the horse comes to the stop smoothly with hind legs under him, front feet together, and head in natural position.

He should be on the track, facing in the direction of movement, and under no circumstances should haunches be displaced to one side or the other. The instant he is stopped, the tension of legs and hands of rider is relaxed. However, *the contact of legs and hands remains as long as the rider wishes the horse immobile.*

To stop on the fixed hand the rider must visualize the bit as a barrier in opposition to forward movement of the horse. The rider's hands maintain strong contact but never pull back. They are *fixed* in position over the withers. The rider's legs and back drive the horse up into the barrier of the bit. The horse reacts by curving the neck, bringing the profile of the head toward the vertical and relaxing the lower jaw. If the rider's hands are truly fixed, the horse is thus himself able to find the reward of relaxation on obedience.

To practice the development of the fixed hand it is first necessary for the rider to establish strong contact with the horse's mouth while his head is in natural position. He now extends both little fingers and rests them on the withers of the horse without moving them. Simultaneously he increases tension by squeezing thumb and fingers. As long as the little fingers do not move from place the hand will be fixed. He is now able to use legs and lower back to drive the horse up to the barrier of the fixed hand. With sufficient practice the fixed hand is maintained without support of the little fingers.

5. Lateral Movements

(a) Leg Yield

(To be done at walk or trot only.) To achieve position, the rider approaches corner of the minor side of the arena and initiates his turn until the horse is at an angle of 45 degrees to the wall. Before head of horse comes closer than a foot or two to the wall and *without losing forward impulsion*, the horse is passed laterally, maintaining a constant position of 45 degrees to the wall. No closer than five meters from the following corner the horse is taken out by curving him into the corner (fig. 110).

The aids for leg yield to the right: The hands maintain strong contact with two direct reins of opposition preventing forward motion. However, the major tension is in the *left* hand. Upper body of the rider is *vertical* and straight but major weight is in right stirrup and on right sitting bone (leading side). Rider exerts strong push with left leg well behind the girth *without lifting heel*! The horse responds by yielding and crossing the hinds. Immediately, the rider shifts tension to the *right* hand which causes horse to cross the fores. This completes one transit. The tension is immediately passed back to the *left* hand. Left leg is ready to repeat for second transit. The aids are continued in a cadenced sequence of steps. In early schooling in snaffle bridle, it will be found helpful to carry the leading hand lower than the off hand by the distance of a fist.

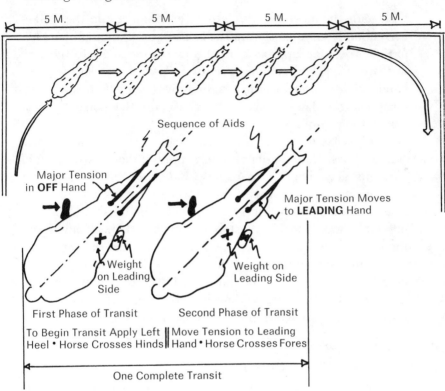

Fig. 110: Leg yield to the right

COMMON ERRORS OF THE LEG YIELD

In the leg yield, as in all lateral movements, the hands and legs of the rider must be coordinated in order to balance each other. This coordination is a subtle thing to teach objectively. It is improved subjectively by *feeling*.

By far the most common error I have noted in the leg yield is the overuse of the rider's left hand when horse is in transit to the right. This pulls the head and neck to the left so that he cannot even see where he is going. The correction obviously is the balance of the rider's hands, alternating tension from one to the other as described above.

If the horse is not between the rider's hand and legs, he

will evade the movement by either (a) running into the wall—
correction is more tension in the reins—(b) swinging haunches
too far to center, approaching at a 90-degree angle to the wall
instead of 45. Correction: less strong use of left leg and left
hand, slightly more leading right rein. (Note that at the 45-
degree angle there is maximum space for the horse to cross
legs without rubbing.)

The horse may also evade by closing the angle to considerably less than 45 degrees and simply proceed to the right
with his neck bent. This usually indicates that the rider is
applying the leg with the heel pointed up. In this case only the
side of the foot comes into contact with the horse and fails to
influence him. The leg must be applied with heel down and
toe everted so that contact is with back of heel or spur.

At first schooling of the horse to the leg yield he may be
permitted a slight bend of the head in the direction of movement. (Never away from it!) When he does learn to yield, he
should execute it with spine straight from poll to dock. Note
that in the leg yield, the horse is moving in one direction only.

(b) Two Track (Half Pass)

All forms may be done at walk, trot, and canter. In all the
following forms of the two track, the horse will now be moving
in *two* directions, forward and laterally, simultaneously.

Fig. 111: Semi-volte at the two track

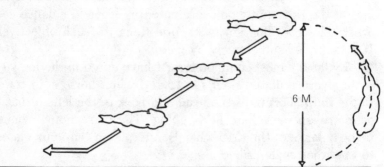

6 M.

1. SEMI-VOLTE AT THE TWO TRACK

This is the easiest form in which to introduce the horse to the two track. The horse is taken from the wall in a semi-volte of six meters. He is then moved forward and laterally, following a diagonal path back to the wall, while remaining constantly parallel to it. The aids to all forms of the two track are similar to those described under leg yield except that the horse is kept in forward motion (fig. 111).

2. INVERTED SEMI-VOLTE AT THE TWO TRACK

Same as above but in reverse. The horse leaves the wall, two tracking out on the diagonal, and returns on the half circle (fig. 112).

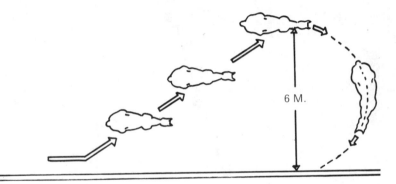

Fig. 112: Inverted semi-volte at the two track

3. TWO TRACK ON THE FULL DIAGONAL

After crossing a minor side the horse departs from a diagonal post and two tracks to the opposite diagonal post. He then continues on to the halfway point of the minor side (A or C), is ridden up the medium line to the other extreme, where he changes hands. He then repeats at the next diagonal post and two tracks the diagonal opposite direction (fig. 113).

4. TWO TRACK ON HALF THE DIAGONAL WITH CHANGE OF DIRECTION

On crossing a minor side, the horse departs from the

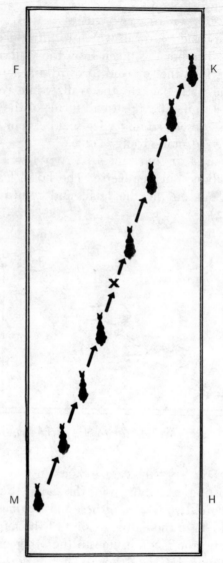

Fig. 113: Two track on the full diagonal

diagonal post at the half pass. Just before reaching the center
of the ring (X) he is allowed to proceed a few steps forward,
then changes direction and two tracks back to the diagonal post

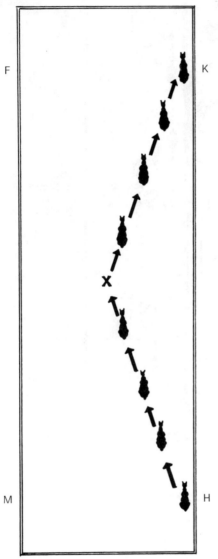

Fig. 114: Two track on half the diagonal

on the original major side. When the horse is sufficiently proficient, he may be put to the change of direction exactly at X, with no straight forward movement permitted (fig. 114).

*Fig. 115: Counter change of hands at the two track on the medium
line*

5. COUNTERCHANGE OF HANDS AT THE TWO TRACK ON THE MEDIUM LINE

Rider turns on to medium line at A. Midway between the first two letters of the major sides he moves at the two track, first to right four steps, then to left eight steps, then to right eight steps, and so on, ending with four steps back to medium line at other end of the ring. The movement may vary by changing the number of steps to either side of displacement. Rhythm should be an even cadence and changes of direction smooth, never brusque (fig. 115).

All of the above forms of the two track should naturally first be perfected at the walk. Only when they can be done satisfactorily at the cadenced trot should they be attempted at the canter.

6. COMMON ERRORS IN PERFORMANCE OF THE TWO TRACK

a. Worst and most common is for horse's head to be bent away from direction of the movement.

Correction: if two tracking to the right, less left hand, more left leg, and more weight in the right stirrup.

b. Spine of horse not parallel to long wall of the arena.

Correction: If forehand is leading, there is too much leading hand; if haunches are leading, there is too much outside leg.

c. Not enough forward movement.

Correction: too much opposition in reins, not enough leg. Note: If horse's forward progress is satisfactory, passive leg at the girth is *off* the horse; if forward progress is insufficient, passive leg closes to combine pressure of *both* legs.

d. Too much forward movement.

Correction: Horse must be put *on the bit.*

6. Turn on the Haunches

In this movement the horse is to perform a large circle with the forehand around a small circle performed by the haunches. The inside back leg of the horse (left back leg when forehand is moving to the left) acts as the pivot and is lifted and replaced in place. The horse's spine remains straight,

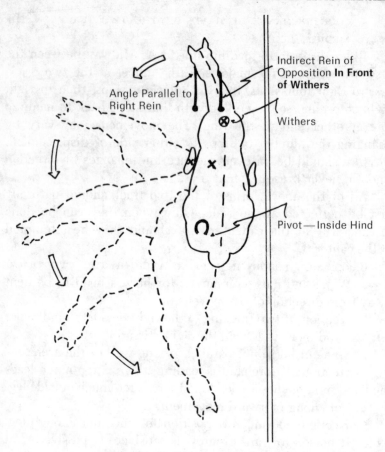

Fig. 116: Half turn on the haunch

though the head may be slightly bent in the direction of movement.

Like the turn on the forehand, this is initiated at the wall of the arena as a half turn on the haunch. When he is proficient at this, the horse may be taken to the medium line and asked for the full turn on the haunch.

Aids are shown in fig. 116 with forehand moving to the left. Right leg is held firmly against the flank, behind the girth, to prevent haunches being displaced to the right. Right indirect rein of opposition in front of the withers balanced by

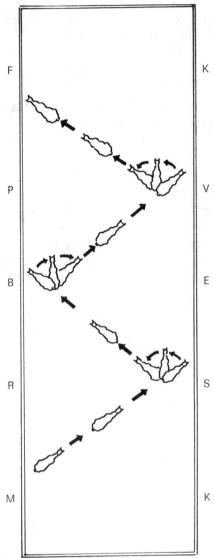

Fig. 117: Broken lines

left rein parallel to it. Rider's weight is on left sitting bone and in left stirrup. Aids are used and relaxed at each step of the horse. At first one may demand only three steps and then reverse aids and return three steps. Later the full half circle of six steps may be demanded.

In comparing the turn on the haunch with the turn on the forehand, one may imagine sitting on a hinged gate. In the turn on the forehand, the hinge of the gate is in front of one. In the turn on the haunch, the hinge is behind one. In both cases we swing the gate. The predominant aids in the turn on the forehand are seat and legs. In the turn on the haunch they are the reins.

(a) Broken Lines

Preliminary training for turn on the haunches. Some horses will encounter difficulty learning the turn on the haunch from a standing position. For these horses it is better to introduce them to the movement by means of "broken lines" shown in fig. 117. Rider starts at diagonal post, riding the figure W shown. At the end of the first leg of the figure W, the rider swings on the haunches, using the aids described above. The hands cause the horse to pause during the swing, but all forward motion is not interrupted. The movement is therefore a quarter turn on the haunch with forward motion. When the horse is executing broken lines satisfactorily, he can be taken back to the wall and asked for the proper half turn on the haunch.

(b) Common Errors in Turn on the Haunch

1. The worst is for the horse to step backward. Correction: less tension in the reins.

2. Irregularity in cadence. Correction: aids must be coordinated and used and relaxed in cadence with the steps.

3. Displacement of haunch. Correction: outside leg behind the girth must stabilize the haunch; upper body of rider must be *vertical* with weight bearing down into the seat.

7. Shoulder-in

Movements described under 7, 8, and 9 are performed with the spine of the horse bent and at walk and trot only. The

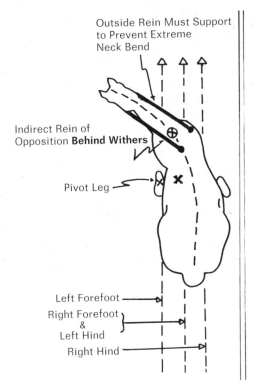

Outside Rein Must Support
to Prevent Extreme
Neck Bend

Indirect Rein of
Opposition **Behind Withers**

Pivot Leg

Left Forefoot
Right Forefoot
&
Left Hind
Right Hind

Fig. 118: Left shoulder-in

purpose of teaching the horse to move with spine curved is to develop him muscularly and to make him flexible.

In the shoulder-in as shown in fig. 118, the haunches of the horse are squarely on the track, parallel to the wall. His spine from that point bends in an even curve to the poll. In order to accomplish this the horse's forehand is brought to the inside track (by flexing the shoulder in). To the person standing on the track in front of the horse as it advances at the shoulder-in, the hind leg next to the wall will leave a track. The inside hind and the outside fore will leave a second track, one following the other. The inside fore will leave a third track. Maintaining this curvature, the horse is induced to proceed straight forward parallel with the wall. There is no crossing of legs involved.

Note: The shoulder-in as performed in the Spanish Riding School of Vienna differs slightly from the above description, which is general practice in the modern world. In Vienna the curvature demanded is greater. It is based on the classical precepts of de la Guérinière, who insisted that the curvature be great enough for the horse to leave *four* tracks.

(a) Aids

The horse in left shoulder-in is curved around the left leg of the rider, which is at the girth. Rider sits with upper body vertical, looking straight ahead. Right leg is behind the girth to prevent quarters from displacing toward the wall. Rein effect is left indirect rein of opposition *behind* the withers. Right hand must give enough support to prevent an exaggerated bend of the neck. Weight is on the inside, or left, sitting bone.

Note that in the shoulder-in, the horse moves toward the outside of his curvature.

(b) Common Errors

1. Horse's spine straight as far as shoulders, with head and neck bent sharply to the inside, thus preventing him from performing a lateral movement.

Correction: more support by passive hand. Active hand lower and farther behind the withers.

2. Horse angled to the wall with straight spine (leg yield in reverse).

Correction: Inside leg is behind the girth instead of at the girth.

3. Haunches everted toward wall.

Correction: more active pressure with outside leg behind the girth.

8. Travers (Haunches In)

In travers the bend of the spine is the same as shoulder-in. But now it is the shoulders that are square to the track and the

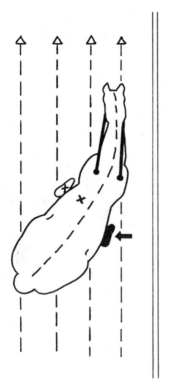

Fig. 119: Travers (haunches in)

haunches curved to the inside track. Again, as in the shoulder-
in, the horse's prints follow three tracks. However, now the
horse is advancing straight forward toward the *inside* of his
curvature (fig. 119).

(a) Aids

The hands act to keep the horse's head straight on the
track. Rider is vertical, looking straight forward. Inside pivot
leg at girth with weight on inside sitting bone. Outside leg
behind girth with pressure to keep quarters to the inside track.

(b) Common Errors

Common errors concern curvature and are quite similar

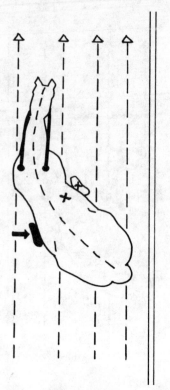

Fig. 120: Renvers (haunches out) .

to those discussed under shoulder-in.

A very difficult maneuver physically for the horse. It should not be overdone.

9. Renvers (Haunches Out)

Physically, the most demanding of all curved spine maneuvers for the horse. Again the curvature of the dorsal spine is the same as in both shoulder-in and travers. The forehand is again square to the wall but now on the *inside track* (fig. 120). The haunches are curved out to the wall and the horse again prints three tracks. Also he is again advancing toward the inside of his curvature.

(a) *Aids*

Identical with travers but reversed.

(b) *Common Errors*

See shoulder-in and travers.

C. GENERAL COMMENTS ONLY ON MORE ADVANCED MOVEMENTS

1. More Advanced High-school Movements

The scope of this manual in terms of detailed instruction has been limited to the foregoing advanced high-school movements. More advanced maneuvers are only briefly discussed below. The reason for this follows.

It has been my observation that any sensitive and ambitious horseman can with patience bring his horse to this level. Beyond this point, to achieve the airs discussed below, one enters a demanding and almost full-time occupation. Should one so wish and be able to indulge oneself, there are more requisites than time. Books that specialize in advanced *haute école* are of course available but will be insufficient. Lacking one's own advanced experience, the aid of a capable dressage master is indispensable. Another fact is that no rider is able to school a horse effectively in advanced airs without previously having experienced these airs on another horse who already knows how to do them. *They cannot be merely imagined!*

To bring a dressage horse to Grand Prix or Olympic level usually occupies a schooling period of five to seven years. The average age at first-time competition of an Olympic dressage horse will therefore usually be a minimum of eleven or twelve years.

In Vienna, the Lipizzan stallion does not begin his education until the age of five, at which time he is usually beginning to change the color of his coat from black to its eventual white. It is believed at the Spanish School that a colt under five does not have adequate power of concentration for serious study.

The entire course of study is considered to be seven years for the horse and an equal time for the rider.

It should of course be remembered that the "above-the-ground airs" in use in Vienna are exhibition airs only and form no part of any international competition. We refer here to such airs as the levade, passage, courbette, capriole, and so forth.

Also worthy of note is the fact that in the Vienna "above-the-ground airs" *all* the stallions do not learn *all* the airs. They are specialists. The stallion who is expert in the levade does not necessarily do the courbette or capriole.

"Heavy dressage" would proceed from the above-detailed movements to:

1. The piaffe.

This is the elevated trot in place without forward motion. It is characterized at its best by high vertical articulation. It is often taught first "in the hand." It is also developed mounted and at times in cavesson between the pillars.

2. The passage.

This is an elevated trot with forward motion with a period of suspension at the highest elevation of each pair of diagonals. It is usually developed out of the piaffe and is probably one of the most beautiful actions a horse can perform.

3. The fully extended trot sitting.

The full extension is extremely difficult to sit on a horse of high displacement. It is demanded only at the highest levels of international competition. All displacement must be taken up in the flexibility of the rider's back.

4. Pirouette.

The full turn on the haunches at a cadenced canter.

5. The change of leg at the canter.

This is demanded at various levels of competition at every four strides, every three, every two, and finally *at every stride*.

As schooling of the above airs progresses, it is essential that the rider begin to refine his aids. The horse begins to refine his sensitivity until he is finally responding to aids so subtle that they are actually difficult for the observer to see.

XVI

Combined Training

Fortunately, there will always be specialization in human endeavors. But specialization arises out of broad basic knowledge and wide experience.

So it is in horsemanship.

The concept of combined training, as demonstrated in the three-day event, is an intelligent recognition of this fact.

In searching for an example of the opposite point of view, I call to mind the following two instances:

I was out riding with an extremely active polo player. I began to discuss horsemanship at length. After listening politely to me for a while, he leaned over and said, "Friend, you are wasting your breath. You see, I am not a horseman; *I am a polo player!*"

End of conversation.

The second example I recall is a series of letters I received from a wealthy man, interested in furthering his young son's career as a jumper. He wanted his son to study for an extended period at the Escuela Ecuestre. He asked me to assure him that his son would jump at least five and a half feet daily, six days a week, during the months of his stay.

I wrote back and assured him that under no circumstances would his son be *permitted* such a routine at the Escuela. I explained that what we taught was *horsemanship* and that we taught it in a balanced way.

End of correspondence.

The rewards of a broad base of knowledge in horsemanship are great. They include the adventures of advanced airs in the dressage ring. They include cross-country riding for both fun and competition. They include steeplechase elements, polo, and the joys of the hunting field in company. They include the thrill of stadium jumping.

In competitive terms, the three-day event is in its Olympic form a most demanding trial. The first day is devoted to dressage, the second to a combination of cross-country, roads and tracks, and steeplechase. The third day is exclusively stadium jumping. However, many less demanding trials of combined training are held throughout the world.

In essence they are simply a recognition of the fact that whatever preference of specialization may exist, the education of both horse and rider should be broad enough to encompass the main resources of horsemanship.

Since there has necessarily been much emphasis in this manual on the work done in the arena, this may be an appropriate place to emphasize that work in the ring must be sensibly balanced with work in the exterior.

The horse forced to work exclusively in the ring finally comes to feel constricted and bored. The rider, too, will come to feel restricted. It goes without saying that a really green rider should first demonstrate reasonable control of his mount in the ring before being sent into the open country on a spirited horse.

The horse who behaves reasonably quietly in the ring may prove to be quite a handful when out in the country with other horses.

What we really wish to do is to apply the skills developed in the ring to the varied problems of the open country, which may well include difficult terrain.

One way of beginning this transition is known as "work on long lines." In a fairly flat area of country we mark out an open arena three times the size of the standard ring. This will be approximately 60 by 180 meters. A tree may serve to mark one corner, a large stone another.

We now repeat the basic patterns of the ring but we are doing them on a scale three times larger. The volte of ten meters will now be thirty! The same precision that prevailed in the ring should now govern work on long lines.

The problems encountered in cross-country riding are many and varied. They may include the jumping of fallen trees, stone walls, post-and-rail fences, and here in Mexico, many types of cactus. They include ascending steep slides and descending steep slides. They may include water hazards that must be jumped over or galloped through. They may include many types of straight banks that must be jumped on and off

The well-planned equestrian school installation will attempt to reproduce as many of these hazards as possible on home ground, where they can be navigated under controlled conditions.

For example, Mexico is a country rich in cactus of many types. Therefore on the training fields of the Escuela we have reproduced many fences of the different types of cactus encountered in the field.

The rider who has worked over rustic obstacles under controlled conditions will have some understanding of collection. He will therefore not allow his horse in the field to race into obstacles extended, with the inevitable attendant dangers.

This is a phenomenon one sees in the hunting field constantly. Here, the problems of cross-country are complicated by the nature of hunting. When hounds are in cry, one must go. One must jump when necessary. One must keep up. The refusal of your own horse may cause the refusal of other horses behind you. At the same time, control is demanded. One does not pass the master! All of this would seem to require some expertise in horsemanship. Strangely enough, many people begin to hunt with only the vaguest ideas of the horsemanship skills demanded. It would seem sensible to learn first to ride capably. Scores of people have come to the Escuela because their experiences in the hunting field have finally convinced them that it is time to learn to ride properly.

It is often revealing to watch a large hunting field either ascending or descending a steep slide. Count the number of riders who know how to go up or down properly.

Fig. 34a shows proper position for a rider ascending a steep grade. Note that the upper body is well forward, heels are down, head of rider to one side of horse's neck looking *up*. The arms are fully extended toward the point of the horse's shoulders, giving him complete liberty of head and neck. Even trotting up a steep incline there will be much motion of the head and neck. At the canter there will be more.

Fig. 34b shows correct position of the rider descending a steep grade. Note that the upper body of the rider is again *forward, not back!* All weight is in the heels. Note difference in position of the arms. The horse that needed freedom ascending now needs *support* on the mouth while descending. At any time during the horse's descent the rider should be able to stop him at will. Cantering up steep inclines is quite sensible, but the *descent should be made at walk or trot* if the angle is steep.

It was my privilege in Madrid to be invited by the Spanish army to the annual ceremony of the descent of the *cortaduras*. This is a field graduating exercise for military students of horsemanship. There are five descents, which increase in height and steepness. The last is a drop of about fifty feet, only a few degrees off the vertical, followed by a rolling hill down into a river. Approach to the edge is at the trot. Descent of the drop is at the walk. The gallop into the river is taken at the end of the drop.

In spite of the fact that the last drop was only a few degrees off the vertical, *every rider was forward.* Putting the weight over the compressed haunch by leaning backward would inhibit the freedom of the haunch to maintain balance by maneuvering laterally.

In a steep descent the horse's hocks are under the haunchlike compressed springs. The haunch must move laterally as each hind advances. The forelegs are braced forward and the horse is further supported by the hands of the rider.

The scope of this manual has been necessarily limited to the essential elements of international riding, as understood by the concept of combined training.

Inevitably, regional and indigenous patterns of horsemanship have evolved that are still with us today. This is more evident in the Western Hemisphere than in the Eastern, for obvious historical reasons. Often the techniques of these indigenous patterns have little in common with the international concept of riding. Indeed, they are often antithetical and serve only to confuse the beginning rider who may sample a bit of this and a bit of that.

In North America, particularly in the United States, there is the tradition of the "saddle seat" for three- and five-gaited horses and a somewhat similar seat for Tennessee Walkers. It exists nowhere else in the world, to my knowledge. It arose originally to fulfill the need of a plantation owner who had to ride all day to the limits of his properties. It hardly has that need today but has become a traditional base for show ring competition.

The United States western seat, also popular in Canada, exists nowhere else to any extent except Australia, where it has been enthusiastically adopted. It, too, was originally a practical working seat for a cowboy who had to run cattle, cut cattle, and rope. Again, the need has largely disappeared, but the traditional form persists, largely as both a "dude ranch" form and the basis for show-ring competition.

In Mexico the "charro" horseman is a national symbol. "Charreadas," which is their form of show-ring competition, are an immensely popular spectator sport all over the country. Since Mexico is far less industrialized than the United States, there is still a great need on small ranches for the *vaquero* seat, which is the basis for charro riding. It is of interest that the whole *vaquero* approach to riding is entirely different from that of his counterpart, the United States cowboy, even though the objectives of work are largely the same. The saddle itself is entirely different, the method of schooling the horse is different, and even the technique of roping is entirely different.

All differing forms of indigenous riding will always be of interest to any enthusiastic rider.

It still remains true that to any man, woman, or child of the modern world, the practice of riding in its international form offers the greatest possible rewards for the practice of either sport or art.

Index

WILSHIRE HORSE LOVERS' LIBRARY

The books listed above can be obtained from your book dealer or directly from Melvin Powers. When ordering, please remit 25c per book postage & handling. Send for our free illustrated catalog of self-improvement books.

Melvin Powers
12015 Sherman Road, No. Hollywood, California 91605

MELVIN POWERS SELF-IMPROVEMENT LIBRARY

ASTROLOGY

ASTROLOGY: A FASCINATING HISTORY P. Naylor	2.00
ASTROLOGY: HOW TO CHART YOUR HOROSCOPE Max Heindel	3.00
ASTROLOGY: YOUR PERSONAL SUN-SIGN GUIDE Beatrice Ryder	3.00
ASTROLOGY FOR EVERYDAY LIVING Janet Harris	2.00
ASTROLOGY MADE EASY Astarte	2.00
ASTROLOGY MADE PRACTICAL Alexandra Kayhle	3.00
ASTROLOGY, ROMANCE, YOU AND THE STARS Anthony Norvell	3.00
MY WORLD OF ASTROLOGY Sydney Omarr	4.00
THOUGHT DIAL Sydney Omarr	3.00
ZODIAC REVEALED Rupert Gleadow	2.00

BRIDGE

BRIDGE BIDDING MADE EASY Edwin B. Kantar	5.00
BRIDGE CONVENTIONS Edwin B. Kantar	4.00
BRIDGE HUMOR Edwin B. Kantar	3.00
COMPETITIVE BIDDING IN MODERN BRIDGE Edgar Kaplan	4.00
DEFENSIVE BRIDGE PLAY COMPLETE Edwin B. Kantar	10.00
HOW TO IMPROVE YOUR BRIDGE Alfred Sheinwold	2.00
INTRODUCTION TO DEFENDER'S PLAY Edwin B. Kantar	3.00
TEST YOUR BRIDGE PLAY Edwin B. Kantar	3.00
WINNING DECLARER PLAY Dorothy Hayden Truscott	4.00

BUSINESS, STUDY & REFERENCE

CONVERSATION MADE EASY Elliot Russell	2.00
EXAM SECRET Dennis B. Jackson	2.00
FIX-IT BOOK Arthur Symons	2.00
HOW TO DEVELOP A BETTER SPEAKING VOICE M. Hellier	2.00
HOW TO MAKE A FORTUNE IN REAL ESTATE Albert Winnikoff	3.00
HOW TO MAKE MONEY IN REAL ESTATE Stanley L. McMichael	2.00
INCREASE YOUR LEARNING POWER Geoffrey A. Dudley	2.00
MAGIC OF NUMBERS Robert Tocquet	2.00
PRACTICAL GUIDE TO BETTER CONCENTRATION Melvin Powers	2.00
PRACTICAL GUIDE TO PUBLIC SPEAKING Maurice Forley	3.00
7 DAYS TO FASTER READING William S. Schaill	2.00
SONGWRITERS RHYMING DICTIONARY Jane Shaw Whitfield	4.00
SPELLING MADE EASY Lester D. Basch & Dr. Milton Finkelstein	2.00
STUDENT'S GUIDE TO BETTER GRADES J. A. Rickard	2.00
TEST YOURSELF—Find Your Hidden Talent Jack Shafer	2.00
YOUR WILL & WHAT TO DO ABOUT IT Attorney Samuel G. Kling	3.00

CALLIGRAPHY

CALLIGRAPHY—The Art of Beautfiul Writing Katherine Jeffares	5.00

CHESS & CHECKERS

BEGINNER'S GUIDE TO WINNING CHESS Fred Reinfeld	3.00
BETTER CHESS—How to Play Fred Reinfeld	2.00
CHECKERS MADE EASY Tom Wiswell	2.00
CHESS IN TEN EASY LESSONS Larry Evans	2.00
CHESS MADE EASY Milton L. Hanauer	2.00
CHESS MASTERY—A New Approach Fred Reinfeld	2.00
CHESS PROBLEMS FOR BEGINNERS edited by Fred Reinfeld	2.00
CHESS SECRETS REVEALED Fred Reinfeld	2.00
CHESS STRATEGY—An Expert's Guide Fred Reinfeld	2.00
CHESS TACTICS FOR BEGINNERS edited by Fred Reinfeld	2.00
CHESS THEORY & PRACTICE Morry & Mitchell	2.00
HOW TO WIN AT CHECKERS Fred Reinfeld	2.00
1001 BRILLIANT WAYS TO CHECKMATE Fred Reinfeld	3.00
1001 WINNING CHESS SACRIFICES & COMBINATIONS Fred Reinfeld	3.00
SOVIET CHESS Edited by R. G. Wade	3.00

COOKERY & HERBS

CULPEPER'S HERBAL REMEDIES Dr. Nicholas Culpeper	2.00
FAST GOURMET COOKBOOK Poppy Cannon	2.50
HEALING POWER OF HERBS May Bethel	3.00

_____HERB HANDBOOK   *Dawn MacLeod*   2.00
_____HERBS FOR COOKING AND HEALING   *Dr. Donald Law*   2.00
_____HERBS FOR HEALTH—How to Grow & Use Them   *Louise Evans Doole*   2.00
_____HOME GARDEN COOKBOOK—Delicious Natural Food Recipes   *Ken Kraft*   3.00
_____MEDICAL HERBALIST   *edited by Dr. J. R. Yemm*   3.00
_____NATURAL FOOD COOKBOOK   *Dr. Harry C. Bond*   3.00
_____NATURE'S MEDICINES   *Richard Lucas*   3.00
_____VEGETABLE GARDENING FOR BEGINNERS   *Hugh Wiberg*   2.00
_____VEGETABLES FOR TODAY'S GARDENS   *R. Milton Carleton*   2.00
_____VEGETARIAN COOKERY   *Janet Walker*   3.00
_____VEGETARIAN COOKING MADE EASY & DELECTABLE   *Veronica Vezza*   2.00
_____VEGETARIAN DELIGHTS—A Happy Cookbook for Health   *K. R. Mehta*   2.00
_____VEGETARIAN GOURMET COOKBOOK   *Joyce McKinnel*   2.00

GAMBLING & POKER

_____ADVANCED POKER STRATEGY & WINNING PLAY   *A. D. Livingston*   3.00
_____HOW NOT TO LOSE AT POKER   *Jeffrey Lloyd Castle*   3.00
_____HOW TO WIN AT DICE GAMES   *Skip Frey*   2.00
_____HOW TO WIN AT POKER   *Terence Reese & Anthony T. Watkins*   2.00
_____SECRETS OF WINNING POKER   *George S. Coffin*   3.00
_____WINNING AT CRAPS   *Dr. Lloyd T. Commins*   2.00
_____WINNING AT GIN   *Chester Wander & Cy Rice*   3.00
_____WINNING AT 21—An Expert's Guide   *John Archer*   3.00
_____WINNING POKER SYSTEMS   *Norman Zadeh*   3.00

HEALTH

_____DR. LINDNER'S SPECIAL WEIGHT CONTROL METHOD   1.50
_____HELP YOURSELF TO BETTER SIGHT   *Margaret Darst Corbett*   3.00
_____HOW TO IMPROVE YOUR VISION   *Dr. Robert A. Kraskin*   2.00
_____HOW YOU CAN STOP SMOKING PERMANENTLY   *Ernest Caldwell*   2.00
_____MIND OVER PLATTER   *Peter G. Lindner, M.D.*   2.00
_____NATURE'S WAY TO NUTRITION & VIBRANT HEALTH   *Robert J. Scrutton*   3.00
_____NEW CARBOHYDRATE DIET COUNTER   *Patti Lopez-Pereira*   1.50
_____PSYCHEDELIC ECSTASY   *William Marshall & Gilbert W. Taylor*   2.00
_____REFLEXOLOGY   *Dr. Maybelle Segal*   2.00
_____YOU CAN LEARN TO RELAX   *Dr. Samuel Gutwirth*   2.00
_____YOUR ALLERGY—What To Do About It   *Allan Knight, M.D.*   2.00

HOBBIES

_____BATON TWIRLING—A Complete Illustrated Guide   *Doris Wheelus*   4.00
_____BEACHCOMBING FOR BEGINNERS   *Norman Hickin*   2.00
_____BLACKSTONE'S MODERN CARD TRICKS   *Harry Blackstone*   2.00
_____BLACKSTONE'S SECRETS OF MAGIC   *Harry Blackstone*   2.00
_____BUTTERFLIES   2.50
_____COIN COLLECTING FOR BEGINNERS   *Burton Hobson & Fred Reinfeld*   2.00
_____ENTERTAINING WITH ESP   *Tony 'Doc' Shiels*   2.00
_____400 FASCINATING MAGIC TRICKS YOU CAN DO   *Howard Thurston*   3.00
_____GOULD'S GOLD & SILVER GUIDE TO COINS   *Maurice Gould*   2.00
_____HOW I TURN JUNK INTO FUN AND PROFIT   *Sari*   3.00
_____HOW TO PLAY THE HARMONICA FOR FUN AND PROFIT   *Hal Leighton*   3.00
_____HOW TO WRITE A HIT SONG & SELL IT   *Tommy Boyce*   7.00
_____JUGGLING MADE EASY   *Rudolf Dittrich*   2.00
_____MAGIC MADE EASY   *Byron Wels*   2.00
_____SEW SIMPLY, SEW RIGHT   *Mini Rhea & F. Leighton*   2.00
_____STAMP COLLECTING FOR BEGINNERS   *Burton Hobson*   2.00
_____STAMP COLLECTING FOR FUN & PROFIT   *Frank Cetin*   2.00

HORSE PLAYERS' WINNING GUIDES

_____BETTING HORSES TO WIN   *Les Conklin*   3.00
_____ELIMINATE THE LOSERS   *Bob McKnight*   2.00
_____HOW TO PICK WINNING HORSES   *Bob McKnight*   3.00
_____HOW TO WIN AT THE RACES   *Sam (The Genius) Lewin*   3.00
_____HOW YOU CAN BEAT THE RACES   *Jack Kavanagh*   2.00
_____MAKING MONEY AT THE RACES   *David Barr*   3.00
_____PAYDAY AT THE RACES   *Les Conklin*   2.00
_____SMART HANDICAPPING MADE EASY   *William Bauman*   3.00

SELF-HELP & INSPIRATIONAL

The books listed above can be obtained from your book dealer or directly from Melvin Powers. When ordering, please remit 25c per book postage & handling. Send for our illustrated catalog of self-improvement books.

Melvin Powers

12015 Sherman Road, No. Hollywood, California 91605

NOTES